Running BOARD MEETINGS

"An entertaining introduction to the game for the neophyte board director."
Financial Times

"Anecdotes, tips and observations for current and aspiring board members."
The Sunday Times

"Not only on target, it's also amusing. A rare combination."
Professor Jay Lorsch, Harvard Business School

"Lively, thought provoking and relevant to directors of enterprises large and small."
Institute of Directors

"A concise, readable, unstuffy and worthwhile book."
Sir Christopher Hogg

"I learnt so much from the text and the humour is terrific."
Jon Foulds, Former Chairman, Halifax Building Society

"This book performs an important service by suggesting a range of useful tips and techniques for making board meetings effective."
London Business School

"Lively and down to earth."
Business Bulletin

"An excellent book."
Financial Director

"His insights into the subcommittees of the board covering audit and remuneration will ring a bell with many non-execs."
London Financial News

"A thought provoking and practical guide to the key steps to running a successful board meeting."
Leicester Journal

"The book's stated purpose is to provoke thought; it also provokes a good deal of (intended) mirth."
The Times Higher Education Supplement

"Provides anecdotes, tips and observations from board members and those aspiring to get the best from their board meetings."
Business in Brief

"A practical, informative and amusing book ... full of wisdom and some great cartoons."
Corporate Governance: An international review

"Crammed with amusing anecdotes and strategic advice."
Business Echo

"A fascinating insight into the workings of that hallowed part of management life."
Wellingborough Herald Post

Running BOARD MEETINGS

3rd edition

How to get the most from them

Patrick Dunne

London and Philadelphia

First published in 1997
Second edition 1999
Third edition 2005
Reprinted in 2006
Paperback edition 2007

120 Pentonville Road
London N1 9JN
United Kingdom

525 South 4th Street, #241
Philadelphia PA 19147
USA

www.kogan-page.co.uk

British Library Cataloguing in Publication Data

A CIP record for this book is available from the British Library.

ISBN-10   0 7494 4974 8
ISBN-13   978 0 7494 4974 2

Typeset by Jean Cussons Typesetting, Diss, Norfolk
Printed and bound in Great Britain by Creative Print and Design (Wales), Ebbw Vale

Contents

Foreword

My predecessor as Chairman of 3i Group, Sir George Russell gave me a copy of *Running Board Meetings* when it was first published in 1997. He described it as a thought provoking and unstuffy book and one which would be of use to directors of businesses and organizations of all shapes and sizes. George was absolutely right and it has been clear from its success that others agreed. The demand for a third edition also proves that there is as much need today.

In his foreword to the first edition George said that:

'The focus on corporate governance in the last decade has delivered some very positive effects. However, we all need to be careful that the debate, the new processes and the substance of what happens in practice remain well balanced. Boards must not lose sight of their real commercial purpose.'

I couldn't agree more and was delighted to be asked to write the foreword for this third edition which has been significantly updated from the second edition which was published in 2000.

So much has happened since 2000 to influence the job of the director in companies large and small. There have been the highly publicized collapses of some major companies across the world. The Sarbanes–Oxley act, the Higgs review, the Smith report and the many reviews of financial markets and corporate governance have also led to a significant increase in the regulation that directors have to comply with and understand.

Alongside this, the expectations that institutional shareholders, the media, government and employees have of their directors has continued to rise – as have the risks of failing to meet these expectations. The legal, financial and reputational risks inevitably are starting to deter some people from taking on public company board positions. Although in some cases this is probably a healthy development, we all need to be careful that the balance of risk and reward is sufficient to attract the best to fulfil these ever more demanding roles.

At 3i we are that lucky the strength and breadth of the relationships we have across the world gives access to some terrific people who meet those defining characteristics of effective directors that Patrick talks about in the book:

'Good judgement, superb interpersonal skills and finely tuned antennae'.

We are also fortunate in gaining enormous benefit from the pioneering work, led by Patrick, that has been done in the area of developing practical board skills. The courses we run for our staff, for the directors of our portfolio companies and the industry as a whole continue to be popular. Boardroom skills can always be developed no matter how experienced you are.

Whether you are an aspirant or highly experienced director I think you will find this book of use; and I am sure you will enjoy reading it.

Baroness Hogg

Acknowledgements

I have been very fortunate to have had the help of so many people in putting together the three editions of this book. I would like to thank and pay tribute to the following:

At home: My amazingly tolerant wife Rebecca. Our three boys who have all contributed. Patrick for his penetrating questions, Nicholas for his great sense of fun and engaging personality and Rory for giving me the natural deadlines of his birth to start the first edition and his first birthday to finish it.

At 3i: It seems a long time since the 'Running Board Meetings' project was begun and so there are a few people I need to thank who have now retired. Our former Chairman Sir George Russell, who gave me not just the benefit of his wisdom but also tremendous encouragement. Brian Larcombe, who was CEO from 1997 to 2004, and Ewen Macpherson, CEO from 1992 to 1997. Two very different characters and two people who taught me a great deal. Richard Summers, my boss at the time of writing the first edition, for being open minded enough to let me have a go. The final retirees are David Wilkinson, Roger Lawson and Eric Barton in the UK, and Frederic De Broglie in France and Gabriel Gutterez Ugalde in Spain for their trailblazing work at 3i as directors of our portfolio companies.

Others at 3i today include our Chairman Sarah Hogg who not only sets a terrific example but whose razor sharp intellect provides tremendous constructive challenge. Brian Larcombe's successor as CEO, Phil Yea, who has skilfully inducted himself into the 3i board. Michael Queen, who now heads up our growth capital business but was Finance Director from 1997 to 2004. Few people I know possess

Michael's wonderful combination of intellect, humility, decency and resilience. Our Company secretary Tony Brierley and his teammate Sabina Dawson have provided excellent advice to me over many years. Sergio Sambonet who runs 3i in Italy and Ere Kariola in Finland, who have both been especially enthusiastic on the subject of developing best practice in their countries over many years.

In my time at 3i in the many roles I have had since embarking on the 'Running Board Meetings' project I have enjoyed some fabulous secretarial and administrative support. I would have to single out Cordelia Brunt, Helen Jones, Karen Wolstenholme, Alex Robb and last but not least Lorene Gibbons. All of them combine great efficiency with charm. The success of 3i's Independent Directors Programme would not have been possible without a great team and I would like to pay tribute to Pat Hayward, Cindy Thorneycroft, Dorothea Kronenburghs in Germany, Jean Louis Grange in France and Bruno Pastore in Italy.

Others at 3i I must thank are Carol Brennan and Charles Richardson.

Wise elders: Sir Adrian Cadbury, Lord Cuckney, Sir Christopher Hogg, Sir Denys Henderson, Lord Alexander, Jon Foulds, Sir Derek Birkin, Raymond Seitz, Sir Max Williams and Tim Melville-Ross know that I mean it with great respect. They all gave me terrific pearls of wisdom at one time or another.

At the Federal Reserve System: Former Secretary William Wiles, current Secretary Jennifer Johnson and Carolyn Doying.

At Leap: Pete Lawson for his wonderful chairing skills, Helen Carmichael, our former CEO, for just being a joy to work with as a trustee and Jenny Rogers, her successor, likewise, and Janet Cummins for setting such a high standard as a board member.

At Harvard business schools: Professors Jay Lorsch and Jay Light.

At Cranfield: Murray Steele, Ruth Bender and Leo Murray.

At INSEAD: Manfred Kets de Vries and Jean Claude Larreche

At UBC Vancouver: Dan Muzyka

Elsewhere in the USA: John Shane, Barbara Thomas, Norton Reamer, Con Hurley, Charles Carter, Alan Ferguson, Peter Bollier, Bob Monks, Hugh Parker, Stan Lukowski, Jeer Thompson and John Ward.

In mainland Europe: Frederic de Broglie, Andrew Richards and Solveig Nyvold.

All of 3i's Independent Directors Programme members: Over the thirteen years I was responsible for this activity we made over 2,000 board appointments through the programme and had tremendous fun as we learnt how to make boards work more effectively all over the world. The members of the programme gave me terrific support and it is unfair to single out any in particular, but I feel I must pay a special tribute to Bernard Norman, Hugh Stewart, Robert Wright, Wayne Bradley and Derek Wooler.

Others who fit no neat category are: Peter Brown from Independent Remuneration Solutions, Sally Field, Janet Morgan, Gerry Acher, David Bishop, Mike Rake and Sean O'Hare.

And finally: John Hawkins, my friend and expert proof reader, Michelle my niece for her cartoons and the Suzy Lamplugh Trust for their excellent guides and work.

Introduction

Why on earth did I decide to write the first edition of this book in 1997? Interest in the subject, arrogance, rampant egomania? Well I suppose all were possibilities. Happily for most things in life you can construct a wonderfully convenient post-rationalisation as to why you did them. This is especially true in business. So perhaps in this particular case, the fact that there was virtually nothing then written already on a subject of importance to all company directors might have moved me in a moment of inspiration, opportunism or pomposity to get scribbling. Coming clean, I was really spurred into action by a series of circumstances.

One of the joys of my job at 3i then was finding chief executives, independent directors and chairmen for companies undergoing significant change. Of most interest were the companies that needed to undergo some dramatic change but hadn't quite spotted or come to terms with it yet. These 'It'll be all right on the nighters' would often say that 'We're really on the edge of something big'. Something big to them meant a business wonderland. Yet in reality it was something really big such as a Grand Canyon style cliff. A good first step in such situations is to attend the next board meeting. Doing this provides a deeper understanding of the issues facing the company and, more importantly, the characters involved in addressing them. As a consequence I've attended many a fun eight-hour session listening to a board discussing the car policy or what type of coffee machines they should have whilst their business runs out of cash. People usually put on a pretty good show for a bit, but normally as long as you are quiet and not distractingly attired they revert to their normal behaviour patterns. These behaviour patterns cover an extraordinary range, and not just for the individuals but for the group as a whole. Few boards, particularly ones that aren't getting on together or are under pressure, can keep up a show for long.

It was after one such marathon session where its length seemed to be in inverse relationship to its result that I wondered 'is there a book on running board meetings that I can give to Fred to help him?' I rushed into the local bookshop the next morning to buy this gift. No luck. Lots on meetings, plenty of sound advice for project meetings and business meetings in general but nothing that really met Fred's need. Fred, I should hasten to add, is a really decent chap who had built a great business and then let it get too much for him. This would have been alright if he had built a strong team around him. Alas, he hadn't. His non-executives were also committing the cardinal sin of not telling him what he needed to hear. This was in no way through fear – it was more because he was such a nice chap they couldn't bear to tell him. As one of them said, 'After all, it's his family's company, not ours.' Result, the wrong people discussing the wrong things in a terribly cosy fashion. Meanwhile the company was in desperate need of radical change.

It did seem somewhat odd to me that nothing much had been written on board meetings so I had a formal literature search done both here and in the USA. Not much again – how puzzling. Board meetings ought to enhance the success of a business and for thousands of companies they do. Yet for many these meetings are viewed as irrelevant, which is bizarre when you consider the amount of effort, cost and stress involved.

With all the discussion and debate over the probity of boards it was worrying me that the important topic of what boards actually do was becoming overshadowed. 'Business is about making money, having fun and doing both in a responsible way.' Yet there was the prospect that they might become considerably less fun. To balance this we had been running a series of case study sessions on board issues with directors of 3i investee companies. Themes included dealing with board disharmony, retaining high quality people, picking independent directors and so on. It was at some of these events that I mentioned my puzzle of there being nothing much available on the board meetings themselves. The reaction was unanimous: do a session on it and write something.

To gather material and ensure that what was going to be written bore some resemblance to the real world, I gathered together groups of 30 to 50 seasoned campaigners for brainstorming sessions and interviewed some well-known masters of the art. The brainstorming sessions included chairmen, managing directors, independent directors and company secretaries from companies big and small, thriving and struggling. A highly sophisticated structure was chosen 'Before', 'During' and 'After'. Quite quickly the importance of preparation and planning came through and we had to assemble more groups on the 'Before'. With this material, a growing collection of anecdotes and the help of the wonderful 3i calendar cartoons, the six-page flyer *Running Board Meetings* was born. Over 10,000 of these were issued. We seemed to have struck a chord.

Case study events for members of our independent director's programme were then arranged. The majority of our then 325 members came. Flushed with this success, we ran identical evenings for 3i investee and potential investee companies. Chemco, the case study we used for the events, is included as an appendix. This is for those of you who want to try it for your board. I have also included a Convo case study on board disharmony. *Directors' Dilemmas*, also published by Kogan Page, contains over twenty case studies with analyses and descriptions of the outcomes in each situation.

Why go on then and write a book? Firstly because enough people whom I respect thought there was a receptive market. Secondly because I thought it might be fun to do it.

Some of the fun was in looking at international comparisons. 3i is a very international business and our research into board structures for our own business and that of our investee companies provided an insight into how things differ in North America, Asia and right across continental Europe. My team of encouragers also encouraged me to go to the United States to see how things compared. American friends and a number of people I'd previously met who sit on both US and UK boards introduced me to a broad mix of US board members. These covered the range from those at fledgling early stage businesses to those at major banks and pension funds. I was also lucky enough to meet William Wiles (now retired) and his team at the Federal Reserve System in Washington. Board meetings at the Fed are about as professional and well organised as you could imagine. Even though most of us don't have quite the same operating environment, the approach they adopt and the rigour they apply to their board meetings is most instructive.

This third edition has been updated significantly to reflect how things have changed in the past Enron and Parmalat era. It also contains a 'rough guide' to the Higgs review of 2003.

My objective in writing this book is nothing more than to provoke thought. There is no universally applicable model or code of practice for running board meetings. One of the fantastic things in business is the variety of situations companies find themselves in. More fantastic are some of the collections of people thrown together to deal with these situations – a sort of corporate Brownian motion I suppose, with thousands of molecules swirling around and colliding into each other, some with a happy union, some with an explosion.

The book has been written for busy people. Each section stands on its own. This combined with a 'Before, 'During' and 'After' the board meeting structure should make it easy for you to dip in and out.

I hope you enjoy it.

Before ...

'The Preparation'

TRIANGULATION

Weird as it may sound, as a kid I was fascinated by triangles and amazed at how useful they were in so many different contexts. I was nuts about aviation and loved to read biographies. Trigonometry seemed so useful to the great aviators like Lindbergh and Bleriot, to pioneering explorers and astronomers and to history's great builders. In my early days in the chemical industry, when I was working on lots of logistical challenges, I would often use triangles to help me work through issues or problems.

When I first started to work in earnest with dysfunctional boards as a venture capitalist, I was learning on the job and felt each situation was quite different. As of course they are. However, combining this with experience of high performing boards I began to recognise patterns and remembered my triangles. It struck me very clearly one day when trying to explain to a very frustrated chairman who had been introduced to turn a business around that pretty well all the issues he had with his board were to do with people, purpose and process, three things.

I drew the triangle below and we quickly worked out that although the board did have people and process issues, before we started anything we had to be sure what we thought the board was for. Only then could we really know that we had a board team fit for purpose and a set of simple board processes to achieve that purpose.

Before embarking on any journey it is helpful to know where you are starting from, where you want to get to and to have some idea of how you are going to get there. I have found my little triangle very helpful

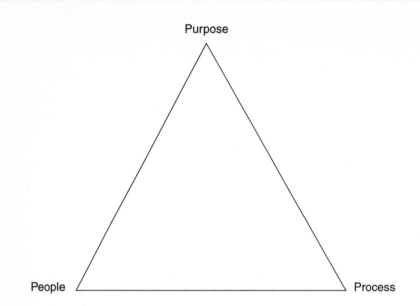

over the years, all over the world, in crystallising thoughts and gaining clarity on what really needs to be done. Not just in a board setting either. It has been tremendously helpful when taking on new roles, especially the ones requiring a major change programme.

WHAT'S THE POINT?

So what's the purpose of a board?

You might expect to get a broadly similar response to this question. You don't. For many it's simply to go through the procedural formalities necessary to comply with the Companies Act and other regulations. So it's all fairly dull and over as quickly as possible with the chairman priding himself that:

'Our board meetings never last more than half an hour.'

For others it's about discussing and taking the key strategic decisions. The ever patient and methodical company secretary or finance director will cover the rest. Perhaps the less enlightened feel it's simply a means of communication with non-executives, joint venture partners, a family that aren't involved in the business or other irritant groups. There's also the occasional chief executive or chairman that thinks it's really the best forum for clearing the in-tray.

Jon Foulds, former chairman of Halifax plc, once asked me:

'Is it a creative process or not?'

The masters of the art that I have interviewed for the three editions of this book seem to broadly agree that for the most part a board meeting is a creative process. 'Why bother having the meeting if it isn't!' For them the point of the meetings is to:

■ agree a strategy and regularly assess its effectiveness;
■ within the strategy establish and maintain clear policy on relevant operational issues;
■ consider and enable successful succession planning throughout the organisation;
■ gain external input and calibration for executive decisons;
■ ensure the company effects all necessary procedural and compliance items across the range from health and safety issues to Stock Exchange compliance matters.

In running training sessions around the world over the past 15 years I have found the following shorthand helpful when describing the role of a board and the purpose of board meetings:

■ *Right strategy*
   Ensuring that the right strategy is in place and that it is being executed. Also ensuring that there is a good process in place for developing and monitoring strategy.
■ *Right resources*
   Making sure that there are the appropriate resources in place to fit with the agreed strategy. The most important of these are people and money.
■ *Keep out of jail*
   By this I mean that the board needs to ensure that the company complies with the appropriate laws and regulations relating to its industry and location. In other words, 'all the governance stuff'.

You would also have to think that a board that had clarity and agreement about what its purpose was would be much more likely to get a better result than one that didn't. Naturally, though, many boards have developed over time without really thinking about what the point really is. After all why should board meetings be that different from other rituals developed over centuries? Considering this fundamental question usually results in getting rid of a lot of the claptrap that clutters up board meetings. It also helps in deciding what people you need. Often as a consequence the requirement for a decent team worrier or administrator in smaller companies will be highlighted. Another typical output is clarification as to what should go on the agenda. Of which more anon.

WHO?

One of the first masters of the art I discussed this subject with when writing the first edition of this book was Lord Cuckney. Well known for running efficient and effective board meetings, I felt he was bound to give me some useful tips. His wide range of experiences in public bodies and major international corporates and his work marshalling the Maxwell Pension Trustees gave him an unusually broad perspective. I expected he would have a huge amount to pass on. I was right.

The most critical thing in his view was to have the right people on the board.

'All the chairing skills in the world are useless if you don't.'

Obvious, I suppose, but who are the right people? Well that clearly depends on the situation. Before you start worrying, there won't now be a complete regurgitation of all that's been written on teambuilding. It is interesting, however, and possibly a bit scary sometimes, when you sit down and analyse what skills, knowledge and experience you need to meet the challenges ahead. If you then look at the skills you have in the present boardroom team you will usually find a few gaps and overlaps, particularly given how quickly things change.

The defining characteristics of great directors, whether they are executive or non-executive, have always been for me:

- great judgement;
- superb interpersonal skills; and
- finely tuned antennae.

You generally make a lot more money and have a lot less bother with colleagues who have a fine sense of judgement of people and commercial situations. However, in order for them to bring those judgements to bear they need strong interpersonal skills. Being irritatingly right

RETIRED EXEC LOOKING FOR AN OFFICE PARTY

frequently means you are not listened to. In order to make great judgements you need to have the right inputs, hence the antennae (see page 28).

Something which struck me as pretty peculiar when first becoming involved in helping people find non-executives was how the previous ones had been chosen. There was one FTSE 100 company that picked a non-executive on the basis of its chairman meeting the individual at a cocktail party. The pair then met the next week for a cuppa and, following a board lunch towards the end of that month which enabled him to meet the rest of the team, his appointment was confirmed. Now of course most chairmen of FTSE 100 companies have to be very good at picking people. This one is clearly inspirational. It also seems odd when you consider that to get into the same company as a graduate there's a fearsome application form, a battery of psychometric tests and role plays together with several days' worth of interviews. Of course I'm not suggesting that any less rigour should be taken in recruiting graduates, though as an aside I do think some overzealous human resource directors have gone a bit far. As a further aside it seems quite important if you are going to have a human resource function that it's staffed with humans who are resourceful. There are many that are neither. Returning to the point it has to make sense to take at least the same amount of care when selecting board members as with other appointments.

For smaller companies it can help focus the mind to consider the cost of a board member in relation to their contribution. Remembering, of course, that sometimes particularly non-executives can be a bit like American footballers – they turn up at each game, may spend most of their time on the touchline but are essential at those vital moments when you need someone to score a major goal.

A piece of wisdom from teambuilding research is that it's no good just picking members in isolation. You need complementary skills and people who can work together. Good chemistry is vital and there must be a balance of perspectives in the team. The saying that 'every business needs a dreamer, a businessman and a son of a bitch' encapsulates this well. It's also possible when constructing your fantasy boardroom team to end up with a board that's too clever or cocky for its own good. That great footballing teambuilder the late Bill Shankly's immortal saying that 'as he had no education he had to use his brains' has given hope to as many as it has prevented others from over-sophistication. Shankly also believed passionately in the principle 'that a highly committed team of average ability players who can work together will outdo a bunch of clever prima donnas any day.'

A board that becomes too comfortable with itself also spells danger. Some element of flux and a mix of ages, sexes and backgrounds is healthy. I think it was JP Morgan who said:

'If two people on a board always agree with each other then one is unnecessary.'

Homogeneity of thought is perhaps why many boards which have hitherto enjoyed a golden period develop feelings of invincibility just at the wrong time.

Chief executives and managing directors today may find their position somewhat lonely and isolated. This is despite the fact that most of the people they come into contact with are terribly nice to them face to face. A sycophant appears for them around almost every corner. In smaller companies where there is only one non-executive, the main reason the MD really wants one is that they want someone to talk to. It can be difficult for even the most open of chief executives or managing directors to share their worst fears or highest hopes with their immediate colleagues. It can be even more difficult sometimes for their colleagues to do the same for them.

The mix of characters on the board will clearly have a big influence on its effectiveness. You might think that its size must do as well. Too big might be too formal – real debate may become inhibited. Too small and the broader perspective could be missed. Small boards are also more prone to become dominated by one individual, although I have to say I've seen many experts from the 'divide and rule' school on bigger boards. The American branch of this school is considered to be much larger because of the tradition of having few executive directors on board, the president/chief executive and chief financial officer frequently being the only two. Ironically many of the outside directors I talked to in the United States felt that this gave the executives more power rather than less. In the worst cases the president was normally the only source of information for the busy outside directors. It is much easier to put your own own slant on issues without any of your other executive colleagues around to give it away in their body language, a point endorsed by Professor Jay Lorsch at Harvard Business School.

The religious difficulty many senior business people had with the separation of Chairman and Chief Executive roles does seem to be waning in the wake of Enron, Worldcom and other big US governance scandals.

IT'S LONELY AT THE TOP

At 3i we have tended to focus on four key board roles, believing that if we get these right then they will ensure the other board members will also be right:

- Chairman
- Chief Executive
- Finance Director
- Independent Director/s.

It is interesting to note that many boards are now moving to a model of having only the Chief Executive and Finance Director as executives on the board. For this model to work the Chairman and the independent directors need to find effective and time-efficient ways to get to know the rest of the senior executive team. Otherwise succession and calibration of information can be tricky.

Because of the way boards evolve, few are the size they are for a particular reason. For most, the reality is that it just happened that way. In the 2003 Higgs Report a census was done of the 1700 or so UK listed companies and some interesting demographic statistics emerged. There were 5172 executive and 4610 non-executive directors on the boards of these companies. Of the 3908 individuals who held non-executive directorships in UK listed companies, 80 per cent had only one post. Ten per cent held two and only 7 per cent held an executive position as well. Thirteen per cent of Chairmen held more than one Chairmanship.

Only five FTSE 100 companies had a joint Chairman but 24 of the FTSE 100 chairmen were formerly the chief executive of the same company. Only 4 per cent of the executive director posts and 6 per cent of the non-executive director posts were held by women. Few boards were bigger than twelve.

There does seem to be a general consensus that a board bigger than twelve forces the board into procedural/governance mode. This is particularly true if there were only four executives or less. I've asked a number of people for tips on this issue of size. A favourite response was from someone who reckoned they knew a board was too big if it needed nameplates at its meetings. In his view it meant they either didn't know each other, couldn't remember who they were, or were possibly a different group each time.

There are numerous studies available on the backgrounds of UK and US board members although they are usually confined to the major companies. Fifty-something males from middle to upper socioeconomic groups still dominate the top group but women are breaking through at last. The rise of the female finance and marketing directors suggests that it will probably be only a matter of time, albeit not overnight, before women are proportionately represented. However, studies in the USA at the Kelly School of Business suggest that the number of women with executive positions in US boardrooms is lower

'He's young ... I don't like that in a man.'

in the late nineteen nineties than in the late nineteen eighties. There are numerous books on the subject. Howeer, as I write this book 3i Group is still the only FTSE 100 with a female chairman.

Overseas nationals are also making an impact and growing in number in many countries. However, there still aren't enough young people being given the opportunity to serve on the board. Of course, no one should be on a board as a token youngster, woman or anything else. They should be there because they are able to add something to the result. There must, however, be the potential to liven up a boat of boards by taking a risk and having a better mix of ages. It is easier to balance a bit of naive vigour than it is to invigorate a tired and out-of-date board.

One group of younger people in Europe and the States who do attain board roles early in their careers are venture capitalists and private equity directors and people responsible for joint venture relationships. It is common practice in the venture capital industry to appoint the director who puts the transaction together as a non-executive upon completion of the deal.

Four reasons are normally put forward as to why it is appropriate for an investing institution to appoint an investor representative to the board:

'Monitoring and influencing investments is easier when you sit on the board.'

'They will add considerable value by bringing a new dimension to the board's thinking.'

'Gaining additional board experience is developmental for the individual investor.'

'In some markets it would be considered as an insult not to do so.'

Some alternative perspectives –

On monitoring and influencing:

'We don't need to be on the board to monitor our investment or enjoy a good relationship with the people we have backed. Experience has enabled us to find more productive ways to keep track of what is happening and to communicate our views on matters of relevance. In fact by not being on the board it is sometimes easier to be more objective and avoid conflicts of interest especially at times of difficulty, when a bid is received or further money is required.'

'It is inherently difficult for any board to strike the right balance between strategic, operational and governance issues. Board meetings that become a show or a talking shop for investors make it even harder.'

On the investor's ability to add value:

'If you developed a specification for what you wanted in a non-executive for a particular situation you'd be jolly lucky if it matched perfectly the guy who happens to be handing over the cheque.'

'Whilst there are many excellent venture capital directors they usually, though not always, are the industry's most seasoned campaigners.'

'I wonder if they might add more value to the investing institution by spending more time on their day job, ie finding, negotiating and managing investments. It is a question of playing to strengths.'

On developing the careers of investors:

'We only want people on our board who are going to do something constructive. Investors might be better developed through board positions in non-institutionally backed businesses.'

On insulting management teams:

'Any management team will naturally be insulted if the investor appears disinterested and is unsupportive. Being on the board may not necessarily make them any more interested or supportive. It will, however, highlight their real level of interest. The guy who turns up late, immediately gets on the phone about another deal and then asks a question covered half an hour before he arrived insults me more.'

The reality today is that most investing institutions in majority-controlled buyouts or syndicate-controlled venture deals will require board membership. The key therefore is ensuring that you get the right person to fulfil the role for your specific situation.

HOW OFTEN?

Most boards meet monthly and for approximately two to three hours. But does this suit the business? For numerous people current board schedules have become the corporate equivalent of a hamster wheel. Fortunately many are now challenging this ritualistic approach and having less frequent but more focused meetings. There is no rule that says you have to have them monthly. At many of the speeches, work-shops and board awayday presentations I've run since the book was originally published I've asked the question: 'Who has monthly board meetings?'

About three quarters of the audience will usually put their hands up at this point.

'Quarterly?'

Typically the balance respond although you always get a few who are either terribly shy, think it's not worthy of an answer or maybe can't remember.

If you then follow up with asking them, 'Why?'

'Because we always have,' tends to be the most common response.

Perhaps questioning this approach would enable boards to focus on the few really big issues to get right and force the many inappropriate items off the agenda which consume so much time and sap energy and interest. Increasing use is made of the board calendar as a way of planning ahead and allocating time appropriately. Sir Christopher Hogg, former Chairman of Reuters, shared this view. When asked about it he said:

> 'I've now retracted from monthly board meetings wherever I can. In fact I'm deeply suspicious of boards that have them. It tends to allow you to waste time and forces focus on monthly reports at the cost of time for strategic issues.'

His preference was for bi-monthly meetings. This view seems to be held by many chairmen, and I know many at 3i were pleased when Sir George Russell reduced the number to seven annually plus a strategy away day. Those who find it too big a shock to the system to go from monthly to bi-monthly in one go may get there in stages, first by moving to nine meetings a year. Sir George, well known for his ability to focus on the basics and concentrate people on what matters, feels pretty strongly about this.

> 'Each board meeting will typically involve an executive board member in three days' work in preparing for it and dealing with the aftermath. Do you really want your top players tied up for 36 days a year with board meetings?'

Tim Melville-Ross, former Director-General of the Institute of Directors, has some concerns about a less frequent meeting:

> 'It's important to meet frequently to build a good team spirit. My experience is that monthly boards are much more use'.

In 2002 the Top Pay Research Group and 3i published a survey of 1200 independent directorships. We received the response shown in Figure 1 to the question: 'How many times a year does the board meet?'

Eight-three per cent of the companies also met for separate budget or strategy meetings. These gatherings are generally held in delightful little sunny spots enjoying the most pleasant of views. Ironically the conference rooms used rarely have windows and little time is given up to enjoy the place. The degree of preparation for such events varies widely. Making them work requires a lot of forethought and effort from the chairman, chief executive and the company secretary.

In a similar survey by Independent Remuneration Solutions in 2005 covering 1200 companies there was more conformity around 8–9 formal board meetings and 2 days for strategy awaydays.

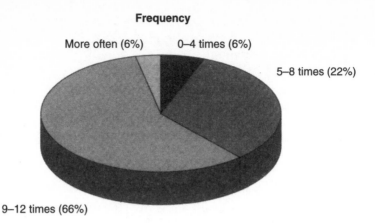

Figure 1   *How many times a year does the board meet?*

HOW LONG?

The effectiveness of discussion will probably vary according to the pressure the Board is under. This is shown in Figure 2.

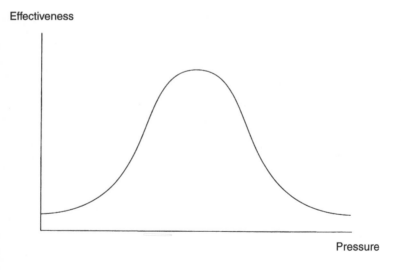

Figure 2   *Effectiveness and pressure curve*

Too little pressure leads to sloppiness, whilst too much can result in hasty and ill thought-through decisions. What are the causes of pressure? Time is an obvious one. Two to three hours was the norm in the companies I talked to who were both happy and effective. The less harmonious and ones with some problems take much longer. As one person told me:

'We have to have a lot of long board meetings to try to put right what we mess up the rest of the time.'

It seems to me to be mad to be overly prescriptive about the length of time a board meeting should take or to suggest that they should always last a uniform time. There has to be a balance.

The Top Pay/3i survey of 1200 directorships in 2002 found the spread of time taken for board meetings shown in Figure 3. Between three and four hours is the average.

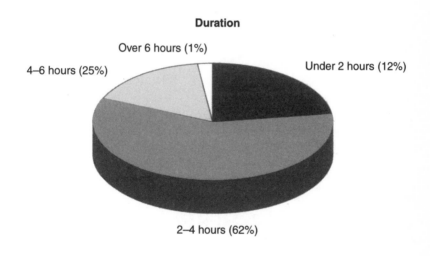

Figure 3 *Time for a full board meeting*

What else causes pressure? Well, it might be easy to think that the company's position must be the main contributor, ie if you're highly successful, it's pretty smug and relaxed; if you're staring a receivership in the face, it must be unbearably stressful. Surprisingly this is often a fallacy. Many of the most successful companies are just as paranoid about falling off their perch. Ever restless, they tend to be continually asking themselves what they're going to do for their next trick. They will on average employ higher quality people so there may be a more competitive environment between board members. Although what I am going to say may not seem right to many, I think the relationships between board members actually cause more pressure than the company's health. Think about the pressure caused in a successful business when someone takes all the credit and the contributions of others aren't recognised. Just look at the pressure caused by searching for a scapegoat when it's not going well. This often prevents a board getting on and sorting out the problem. Conversely many overcome some horrendous external shock or threat because they are well led and galvanised into action. Rates of change in the sector, the prevailing economic climate and a whole host of other obvious factors will also raise pressure. The major components, though, are people or issues you can't stand, a vicious cocktail of 'no point, no action, no fun', or worse, a ritual beating or bleating.

An interesting exercise is to ask each board member to put a mark where they think the board is on the effectiveness and pressure curve in Figure 2. You may find some surprisingly different points of view. Yet more instructive is to go a step further and ask those not on the board to mark where they think the board is. The chairman normally thinks his board's about three-quarters of the way up the left-hand side of the curve. Analysts or investors often think the board is only half-way up the same side (ie: fat cat territory). Meanwhile, the employees and frustrated customers or suppliers would put their mark way over on the right-hand side (ie: the land of the headless chickens). The power of 'seeing ourselves as others see us' is, as ever, especially useful.

WHERE?

Companies sometimes have a preference for holding meetings at locations other than their head office, perhaps a subsidiary location or overseas operation. There are mixed views on the wisdom of this approach. If the objective is to inform the board about a part of the business or meet the people, is this the best way to do it? The diversion of effort to a subsidiary location can be significant, the cost high and the logistical challenge over-demanding. Many board members and particularly canny independent directors may find visits of a different nature more useful for obtaining a deeper understanding.

WHAT ABOUT THE BOARDROOM ITSELF?

At one board more than slightly reluctant to accept change, I was sat down at a very cramped table and introduced in the following way: 'And now we're going to hear why we need another non-executive.' He might as well have added 'from this clever dick sitting on my right'. This was approximately three hours into the meeting. Regrettably we were only half way through the agenda. Perhaps the cramped seats or maybe the boredom led to my somewhat aggressive response: 'I'm terribly sorry. I thought I was here to talk about replacing non-executives, not adding more. Anyway the table's not big enough for anyone else.' Suddenly the three septuagenarian non-executives sat bolt upright in their chairs. One of them rather supportively from my point of view said: 'The lad's right you know, we can't afford a new table.'

Boardrooms obviously must suit their purpose. Light, airy and erring on the cool side seems to represent a general preference. As is an uncramped, dark and highly polished table which is wide enough and not creaking. A good measure of wide enough might be 'where you can't kick the person opposite'. Some, however, prefer a horseshoe shape facilitating the use of visual aids for those presenting to the board. In choosing this style you need to be careful not to lose some of the intimacy of the oval approach.

With regard to temperature you can always borrow the well-known airline hostess trick of turning the heat up or down to get the passengers asleep or awake at the right time. Not having the plugs, projectors, light and other basics in the right place also crops up surprisingly frequently as a minor irritant.

Of more importance are the chairs – comfortable, but not soporific, quiet and certainly not those 'slippy hot ones' or the terribly low ones which make shorties like me end up with our chins where our elbows should be. Deciding where people sit is another issue. Should they always sit in the same place? You also need to avoid interruptions, welcome though they occasionally might be. In summary it's important to get all the domestic arrangements right otherwise 'people can waste a lot of time moaning about the coffee' or worse, can become downright grumpy.

WHERE TO SIT?

In smaller companies with three or six board members this clearly isn't an issue. When the numbers are greater where people sit can affect the effectiveness of the meeting. Figure 4 shows a model which seems popular amongst boards of around ten. Don't forget though that quite a lot of grown ups, particularly those possessing moderate egos, aren't always comfortable with being told where to sit. Just as many people prefer the random method as those with a passion to plan as much as possible.

Figure 4   *Where to sit?*

The seating plan in Figure 4 has been designed with the following in mind:

- The chairman and the deputy chairman should have a complete field of view, almost windscreen-wiper like.
- They also should be opposite each other for increased 'winkability'.
- The company secretary should be between the chairman and the finance director to provide papers and prompts when required.
- A chairman always has their back to the window. Being opposite the door they can see all comers and goers.
- The chief executive sits next to the chairman to emphasise unity.

- To avoid the non-executives sitting as a group, a noughts and crosses method has been used to mix them up with the remaining executives.
- For convenience keep the positions of the chairman, deputy chairman, chief executive, finance director and company secretary the same at each meeting but change the positions of the rest.
- If you have a board lunch before or afterwards have completely different positions.

WHAT INFORMATION BEFOREHAND?

Many famous disasters including the Charge of the Light Brigade have occurred because of erroneous information. Many more have been made on the basis of no information. It's clearly vital for a board to get the right information at the right time and in a form it can digest at appropriate speed. The right information appears to be accurate and concise fact, ensuring the directors know the current and most likely future position of the company, plus enough supporting information to enable proper debate and decision on discussion items. The right time appears to be at least a week ahead of the meeting, but not so far ahead that too much time is spent at the meeting providing updates.

The right manner is in short succinct reports with as much represented graphically as possible and the real issues made abundantly clear. Using colour coding so that different items are always easily picked out is also popular, ie agenda white, financial papers always in yellow and so on. Beware, though, because quite the prettiest board papers I've ever seen turned out to be the most misleading. There's something magical about a computer-generated graph that takes many of us in. Changing the format from meeting to meeting whilst carefully avoiding confusion or generating suspicion can provoke a better understanding. Some boards now use pre-board briefings for those not up to speed on a particular issue. This obviously needs care as it can be used as an excellent way for an overly autocratic chief executive to get the right answers from the board.

So what is the typical length of board papers and what do they consist of in effective and happy boards?

The regular items usually consist of:

- *an agenda* (one page – you know you've got problems if there are more);
- *minutes from last time* (two or three pages);
- *management accounts pack* (ten pages);
- *papers relating to specific agenda items* (anywhere from 1 to 20 pages each).

An amusing fact emerged when I was researching this area. When asked what they consider to be the ideal length of board papers in total for a meeting, most chairmen gave me a number half the size their own were in practice.

A good company secretary will guide a novice in preparing a board paper on a specific item, giving useful advice as to the format, length and style required. In looking at board papers used by a whole range of companies a typical profile of 'Purpose', 'Background', 'Issues' and 'Recommendations' was clear.

WHEN SHOULD BOARD MEMBERS RECEIVE THESE PAPERS?

Most boards circulate papers a week in advance of the meeting. However, I do remember being chastised by one managing director for introducing 'a hopeless independent director'. His complaint was that the board's latest member hadn't read his board papers before the meeting. Worse, this was the second time it had happened. I was particularly concerned by this as it seemed most unlike the individual concerned who in my view was a highly diligent character. Perhaps the papers were just too long or not relevant? I diplomatically enquired whether this was the case. 'Of course not,' came the response. So I asked, 'Well, when did he get the papers, he wasn't away on holiday was he?' 'No, of course not, they were at reception for him to collect as normal just before the meeting.' You will no doubt be thinking that the independent director is still at fault for allowing this to happen. You're right. In the early 'getting to know you' stages of a new appointment this is an easy trap to fall into, especially when trying to build a rapport. Hindsight usually suggests though that is is well worth the pain and the risk of upsetting the relationship at a delicate stage to set the tone and establish the ground rules. By using a clear appointment letter from the company to the independent director this and other related pitfalls can be neatly avoided. A copy of a menu-style appointment letter is included in Appendix III.

HOW DOES A BOARD CALIBRATE THE INFORMATION IT IS PROVIDED WITH?

'The addition is correct, Wilkins, but where is the money?'

Of course there are some canny operators who have an uncanny knack of knowing when the most eloquently presented and well researched proposals just don't make sense. Getting the green light – sorry, gaining board approval – for a new product launch or major capital project is where these people prove invaluable. Their most telling questions tend to be 'Who says?' 'What are the competition working on?' 'Why will anyone buy it?' 'Who's building/supplying it?' 'Do they know what they're doing?' and my favourite 'But what's it for?'

9-5

'I find it simply amazing that what we know as just good business is perceived by the public as greed.'

Even if you are lucky enough to have a board of innately shrewd operators it is still vital to get your perspective right. In this situation the 'who says?' question proves particularly powerful. Questions which focus on the way in which the research, market or otherwise, has been conducted can also produce amusing responses. Most of our decisions are still based upon too much internal information and not enough calibration with the real world. The rapid rise in corporate tourism and the greater degree of openness these days is an interesting and healthy development. People love talking about their business, especially if it's successful. We all have learned the power of 'talking to our customers'. Some have even listened. The really smart people have also avoided giving them questionnaire fatigue in the process. I am not sure, though, that we have gone quite as far along this learning curve with suppliers, customers and employees. We often have an unrealistically high or low view of them and it may be far too general and not based on any real hard fact. Independent directors can clearly bring experiences from the other situations they are involved in. What surprises me is how few boards have other external visitors to broaden their view.

Another increasingly critical area relates to decisions made on major investments in information technology. In a sense this is back to who sits on the board. There is bound to be considerable anxiety over the big IT decisions. We are always anxious when the importance of a decision is high and our understanding of the subject is low, since the whole of the business will know if we've got it wrong. Most of us are also naturally suspicious of the IT salesmen and consultants whose advice is laced with vested interest. Surprising then that so few boards ensure they have enough IT awareness amongst the boardroom team and they receive so little IT training. By implication most IT decisions are really taken by the IT director who is often the finance director as well. We then sack them when they get it wrong. The sacking makes us feel less guilty but the business is still left with the same system. This is not to suggest that the whole of the board should become computer freaks or nerds, merely that they need to be aware of the possibilities and the risks in a bit more depth. Growing numbers of business people at all levels are visiting other companies to see their systems in operation – another healthy trend.

A large amount of time is spent in producing analysing and reading board papers in the belief that they are the key input to a fundamental decision. As a consequence there is little chance of the average board member running out of reading material. Yet for many it is what they hear before, during or after the meeting that will really drive their thinking, not what they read. Having the discipline to go through the process of writing a detailed board paper providing an analysis of options, costs, risks and rewards on a subject ought to be useful. What matters is not necessarily what you see written before you but the rigorous process the operators have had to go through to persuade. There is, however, a dilemma here in the word processor, spreadsheet driven, multi-media age we live in. When canvassing views of people on this subject there was considerable support for the more disciplined approach from board members. Less so from the producers of such reports. Funny that. A slightly paternal or matriarchal feel emerged – board members complaining that this will hurt us more than it will hurt you and so on.

Although they were in a very small minority several people I talked to who were just below main board told me some slightly disturbing things. The most extreme of these said:

> 'It didn't matter what the facts were. As long as you put it in a form the old buffers could easily digest, they would approve what you wanted. They never argued with spreadsheets or computerised graphs – only opinions. So the trick is to work your opinions into a chart or a spreadsheet assumption.'

If there has been research conducted externally there is sometimes a debate as to whether it's better to give board members the originals or summaries produced by executives. A fair number of independent directors I know prefer the originals – suspicious lot. When asked why, they usually said that they were suspicious of the quality of consultants in general and felt that seeing the real work gave them a much better feel for the rigour and professionalism – thus giving them a feel also for how much weight these views should carry. My observation on this topic is that a huge amount depends upon the trust in which board members hold each other both in terms of honesty and competence. To try to generalise is dangerous. If you can't trust the executives to pick decent consultants then perhaps a deeper problem exists.

'Talk to a few peasants! You might learn something!'

This cartoon is not meant to be derogatory in any way or to show that a CEO is a modern day king or queen cocooned in their own little magic kingdom with boardroom colleagues. However, it is generally true that most board members live in a slightly different world to the majority of their customers and employees. Keeping a grip on the real world is tricky. The only way for many is to have regular doses of it. This doesn't just mean buying a tabloid newspaper every day, it means talking – and more importantly listening – to people at all levels and places inside and outside. In most of the really serious underperformers you tend to find a better idea of what the problems are and what needs doing to fix them from the most junior employees. Rule number one for most turnaround experts is firing the company prat. This is the person, usually fairly senior, who has no respect amongst customers or staff. Dizzy with their meteoric progress, they don't really know what they're doing and, what's worse, they can't stop doing it.

WHAT PRE-DISCUSSION SHOULD TAKE PLACE?

'So you would say your imminent failure is all down to the Finance Director you chose then'.

A thorny issue for chairmen is how far they should go in shaping discussions before the meeting. There is a broad consensus that chairmen should be extremely well prepared and they should sound out other directors before the meeting on contentious matters. They must, however, avoid 'putting the muscle on' or 'leading the witness'. Some chairmen pride themselves on the fact that they can and do write the minutes before the meeting and seldom have to change them. What, then, is the point of the meeting?

Sir Derek Birken, former Chairman of RTZ, had a clear view on this. He told me in his wonderfully direct and robust way that:

'I've no time for all this pre-meeting and sounding out stuff or for political boards. The chairman's job is to ensure there's an atmosphere of trust and cohesive team.'

Interestingly, Sir Christopher Hogg is of like mind:

s to develop the company, which is far
between executives and non-execu-
it is about spinning endless webs of
e assumption that evil will otherwise

ON THE AGENDA?

ou've assembled the right people.
to me as 'really the most difficult
rt is obtaining the right balance
ssues. For many debate tends to
gure 5 in terms of time and focus,
ition.

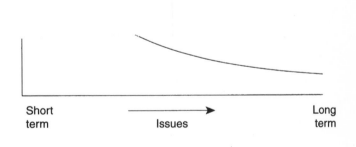

| Short term | | Issues | | Long term |

Figure 5   *Time/focus curve*

Most boards really have only six or seven key things to get right each year. Yet few of us really take the time to sit down in advance and decide what these are likely to be and then allocate the board's time accordingly. It can be very difficult to figure out what these six or seven things are in advance. There will inevitably be at least one major event during the year which alters the board's priorities. Hiding behind this excuse can be easy but there is considerable benefit to debating and gaining agreement as a board on what the critical issues are.

In underperforming companies you often find that one of these key items for the board to get right is strategy. At one board where I was asked along to see if they needed a non-executive it quickly became crystal clear that the company didn't have a strategy. They were really in three quite distinct businesses. Unfortunately they believed they were only in one. There was a strong belief that they had no competition because no one competitor spanned their complete product range. They did, however, have fierce competition in each segment.

At a suitable moment in the meeting the chairman turned to me and said: 'You've heard our debate this morning and met us all. Now tell us what on earth a non-exec could do for us.' My reply was that it would be arrogant on the basis of a couple of hours to give a detailed response but it did seem to me that someone objective might help develop the strategy. I was careful not to say 'get a strategy'. 'What the hell are you on about?' he said, obviously warming to me. 'The strategy is perfectly clear to all of us and we're in complete agreement on it, aren't we?' There was a rather helpful 'Um yes', 'Well kind of' response from the others, enabling me to suggest: 'An interesting experiment, perhaps when I'm gone, is to quickly go round the table and each say what you each believe the company's strategy to be.' A wry smile came from the finance director. Unfortunately the chairman noticed and pounced. 'Good idea. Let's do it now, Jim [the hapless Finance Director], you go first.' Sad but true, each of the six board members then gave a completely different strategy covering the whole range of possibilities.

Talking about strategy can be a lot more fun than ensuring the business is properly under control. So boards that spend too much time on strategy and not enough on ensuring operational policies are appropriate can easily become unstuck. Striking the balance is an art that excellent chairman develop and nurture. Sir Derek Birkin felt strongly that if:

> 'A board has the right strategy then you find that operational matters don't consume too much time at board meetings. This is because major capital expenditure approvals, policy matters and so on will just naturally fit. If they don't then you need to revisit the strategy.'

A minimalist gardener, Sir Denys Henderson, former chairman of ICI plc, notes:

'You don't pick a plant up and look at its roots every six months. Strategy is a bit the same. You have to take your time to get it right and then avoid tinkering with it unnecessarily.'

Spending your time on what matters will help you to avoid feeling like the chap signing above. Sadly what matters is not always what you enjoy so this can be difficult to achieve in practice, particularly for an expansionist board full of gusto.

So what does a typical outline agenda for a high performing company look like?

AGENDA

Approval of previous Minutes and
Matters Arising

Formal approvals of matters requiring limited
discussion

Executives' Reports
    Chief Executive
    Finance Director

Operational Policy Issues

Strategic Issues

Any Other Business

This order is typically chosen so that the operational, procedural and compliance type issues can be quickly dispensed with enabling ample time for the more important and enjoyable strategic items. However, if you adopt this approach and then go back and look at what time was actually allocated to the strategic issues you can easily get frustrated at what little time was really spent. An excellent chairman will of course minimise the time spent on subjects which can be dealt with by pre-reading and committees of the board. The really excellent chairman will also ensure that people have pre-read and do understand what is being approved.

One trick I have used is to jot down on the agenda before a board meeting how long each agenda item should take, then to the right how long I expect it to take, then to the right again how long it did take. If the chairman and I are getting on well I'll ask him how long he thought we spent. There is usually quite a difference between these four sets of times. The comparisons can be instructive.

If you having problems spending enough time on the strategic issues one technique to try is to switch the order of the operational and strategic issues for discussion to alternate board meetings, ie discuss the strategic issues before the operational at every other meeting. If you are having very severe problems, try skipping the executives' reports occasionally as well. When looking at the proportion of time taken by individual items the executives' reports are the ones which often take the longest and which people – especially the CEO – think takes much less time than they actually do. A technique used by John Foulds, former Chairman of the Halifax Building Society, to set expectations is simply to jot down the time anticipated for discussion beside each agenda item.

Another technique used by larger organisations where the nature of their business requires board approval of a high volume of operational items is to split the agenda in two. The first part, the 'summary' agenda, is for items requiring approval but no discussion. This is then followed by a 'discussion' agenda. The most sophisticated use of this I came across was at the Federal Reserve System which of course has the additional delight of holding a number of meetings open to the public. Only a tightly defined group of matters are allowed onto the summary agenda. A review process ensures that there is a relevant split between summary items and those brought to the board for discussion. This approach is found to be highly effective in large organisations and can easily be adopted in smaller companies.

For those fascinated by the subject of what might be the ideal number of items to have on an agenda, when the Top Pay Research Group and 3i did their 1999 poll of 1418 companies they found the range shown in Figure 6. I suspect little has changed since.

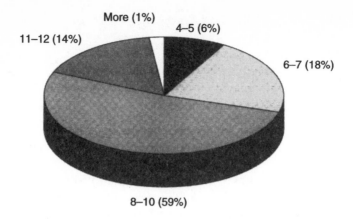

Figure 6   *How many items on the agenda?*

WHO SHOULD SET THE AGENDA?

Usually the chairman and the company secretary set the agenda. The company secretary focuses on the legal and compliance issues, the chairman on everything else. Most boards allow any board member to submit items for consideration by these two. In practice the chief executive will also have significant input and be shaping the chairman's thinking.

WHAT IS ALLOWABLE UNDER 'ANY OTHER BUSINESS'?

This was an issue of concern to several of the company secretaries I spoke to. One had a simple definition:

> *'Anything for which a board view or approval is essential, that can't wait until the next scheduled board meeting and only arose as an issue worthy of board attention since the board papers were dispatched. However, certainly not the approval of an acquisition that hasn't had discussion at a previous meeting.'*

One other finance director whom I mentioned this to said:

> *'If only we'd had that rule there'd be at least ten dog companies we wouldn't have bought.'*

AWAY DAYS

If there are approximately 1700 companies listed in the UK and on average they spend two days a year on board away days then that is 3400 days spent by each of the 5200 executive, 4600 non-executive and 1700 chairman taking part. Thirty-nine million days. And that's just listed companies.

So a lot of senior and expensive resource is committed to this form of meeting. But how effective is the away day format? I hear very mixed views. Some find them highly effective and absolutely essential in ensuring the company has the right strategy. Others find them an energy-sapping, expensive chore which has no positive effect on the company at all.

A few years ago when I was writing a play on strategy I tried to see if there was any best practice guidance published on running away days. To my surprise I couldn't find any. So I rang around the business schools to see if they had done anything on this. As many business school professors facilitate away days I thought they were bound to have something on it. Sadly, there was very little. Only my good friend Murray Steele at Cranfield had written something. Together we talked about this and then I informally canvassed the views of a wide group of directors to see what their experiences of away days were. In summary the response was 'mixed'.

What were the issues for those who felt their away days were ineffective? There were several:

- lack of clarity about the objectives for the away day;
- over-ambitious agendas;
- inadequate preparation;
- no follow-through post away day;
- poor choice of venue;
- weak external facilitation;
- over-dominant chairman or chief executive inhibiting real debate;
- over-dependence on finance director to do all the work beforehand;
- getting the executives out of functional or business line representative mode;
- personal agendas inhibiting open debate;
- poor experiences for non-board members attending;
- away days becoming ritualistic and too easy.

So Murray and I produced the list of tips below:

- Be clear on the purpose of the away day and your desired outcomes. (e.g. selection from a number of well-researched strategic options).
- Decide early enough whether to use an external facilitator and if so select one relevant to the issues being discussed who will do the necessary homework.
- The chairman or CEO should brief the facilitator about the team dynamics, politics and taboo subjects. (the facilitator will then have to interpret skillfully!).
- External facilitators, if used, need to be credible with executive and non-executive directors; they are not there to lecture but to facilitate. They must be prepared to challenge the chairman and chief executive in the same way as they are prepared to challenge other directors. They must be able to maintain an objective and neutral approach but also be engaged and have a clearly defined process for running the day which combines an element of flexibility. Finally they have to assist the chairman in generating the right atmosphere.
- Decide whether there will be non-board members present and if so brief them appropriately.
- Hold the away day offsite.
- Don't allow interruptions except in case of emergency.
- Don't start with an operational board meeting.
- Participants should be prepared to challenge each other, in particular to surface differences – a key to success is the quality of debate, both in content and challenge.
- No one has a monopoly on wisdom so no one should dominate the debate.
- Responsibility for implementing actions arising should be clear.
- Follow up and review the effectiveness of the day as part of your annual board review.
- Finally, the 'socialising' of the board is an important part of building a strong and cohesive board, so ensure that there is sufficient emphasis and time devoted to this.

BOARD CALENDARS

Historically the board calendar was just a list of dates, times and venues for the board meetings for the coming year. Increasingly companies large and small seem to be making much more sophisticated use of this simple planning tool. They seem to be used to:

- ensure specific items are discussed at the appropriate time;
- provide time for sufficient preparatory work to be performed;
- make sure the less interesting, routine but essential items are not forgotten about;
- remove clutter and avoid repetition of discussion.

Any calendar must be considered to be a plan and not something cast in tablets of stone. Issues will inevitably emerge during the year which are of significance to the board and which require considerable thought and discussion. It is sensible therefore not to overcrowd the calendar. Many Company Secretaries seem to have this off to a fine art and plan two years in advance which seems to balance rigour and flexibility.

An example of a calendar for a medium sized private company is provided with the CHEMCO case study in Appendix I.

The calendar overleaf is a fairly normal one for a plc.

January

29	11 AM	Remuneration Committee – Strategy Review
	2 PM	Board

February

26	10 AM	Environmental Committee

March

19	11 AM	Audit Committee – General View
	2 PM	Board

April

16	10 AM	Remuneration Committee – 1997 guidelines

May

4	2 PM	Regulatory Committee
20	6 PM	Board Cocktail function for key shareholders and customers
21	9 AM	Remuneration Committee – Review Executive Directors
	11 AM	Audit Committee – Annual Accounts
	2 PM	Board

June

2	6 PM	Accounts Board Committee
8		Preliminary Announcement of Results
16		Annual Accounts posted to shareholders

July

9	11 AM	Annual General Meeting
	2 PM	Board

October

1	9 AM	Audit Committee Annual Report
	2 PM	Board
13	*Evening*	Strategy Away Day
14	*All Day*	

November

3	2 PM	Environmental Committee
19	9 AM	Audit Committee – Half Yearly Accounts
24	2 PM	Board
25	6 PM	Accounts Board Committee – Half Yearly Accounts
26		Interim Statement

December

6	10 AM	Regulatory Committee
17	*Evening*	Staff Christmas Party

HOW IS THE RIGHT ATMOSPHERE CREATED?

Let us suppose that you have managed to assemble the boardroom team of your dreams. You are also lucky enough to have the ideal room to hold your meeting in. Your agenda is perfectly pitched and there is a model set of accompanying board papers. What else can you do to maximise the chances of having an excellent board meeting?

Engendering an atmosphere of energy, purpose. seriousness and trust will be a natural objective for any thoughtful chairman. They will know they are getting it right because their boards enjoy and value the board meetings. The chairman's role during the board meeting is discussed in more detail later. But what can be done before a meeting takes place to ensure there is the right atmosphere?

Boosting the team spirit through extra curricular activities is an established method. Inviting the independent directors along to social events for customers, suppliers or staff is another. An independent director who is a real master of this art was Sir Max Williams. Sir Max, a former deputy chairman of 3i, has long been at the top of people's invitation list for such events. His perfect blend of charm, humility, brains and good humour have added much to the 3i board spirit over the period he was a director. Moreover, our customers and staff would come away from such events not only being impressed by him but with a feeling that we had genuine humans on the board. Showing humility can be difficult. It may not come naturally to all on a board. Having a seasoned campaigner like Sir Max around helps set the tone for the rest.

Board dinners on the eve of a meeting are popular especially amongst those who hold their meetings in locations where people will need to be there the night before. However, not everyone is smitten with this idea. Some I spoke to felt that this was the worst thing you could do with a bunch of workaholic fifty- or sixty-somethings. When I asked one of them why the reply was:

'Well, staying up way past your bedtime and having more to drink than normal after a long journey doesn't exactly make for a perky contribution the next morning does it?'

Another believed that the scheduled dinner the night before can inhibit some of the best independent directors taking appointments because of the logistics. He said that:

'The logistics can sometimes make a nice idea impossible. It is better to get the right people there for when it matters than to have some of the nicer refinements.'

The logistical challenges for board directors whatever the size of the company can be high but if you can arrange it so that you can travel together it can be productive. There is nothing quite like a long journey together to build on a good developing relationship or to crystallise your decision to end a poor one.

*'The meeting is going to require great delicacy. Just between us,
I'm glad we didn't bring Rayburn along.'*

Having someone responsible for complacency avoidance is another essential role. As Raymond Seitz says:

'A bit of worrying does you good.'

One of the things he thinks that it is important for a new independent director to do is:

'To figure out what they do worry about and what they should worry about.'

'You must also avoid being frightened by your own shadows and becoming paranoiac.'

A board that can balance its sense of seriousness and purpose with a good sense of humour can enhance a business's performance considerably. Many of the masters of the art of chairmanship possess a keen sense of humour. Few of them are perceived as clowns or would tolerate court jester types for long.

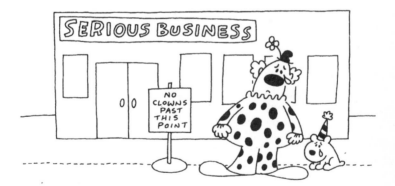

Family companies have an atmosphere all of their own. The history of the family and those deeply personal interrelationships generated from the shared trauma and joy inevitably reach into the family company boardroom. When talking about succession in family companies at an event in Leeds one night I said:

'It must be terribly difficult to be objective about people you love.'

A classic Yorkshire tyke from the back was then heard to say:

'Aye, I know, it can be even harder if you hate them to death.'

One family company chairman I know who has been tremendously successful but plays his cards very close to his chest is wrestling with this issue of succession at the moment. He has two offspring both of whom are being groomed for potential succession. Both have been trained well, have had periods outside the business and are generally considered to be of high potential. The father very proudly told me recently that although he had absolutely no intention of retiring for years he had finally decided who would succeed him should he fall under a bus. 'Who?' I rather nosily enquired. 'I'm not telling a soul, not even Joan (his wife), and I'm certainly not putting it in the will. I don't want arguing over that.' 'So how will anyone know who it is?' 'Errrrr.'

Communication is always more difficult when emotional sensitivity is high.

'Your mother just called to remind you she owns controlling interest in this company'

SOME INTERNATIONAL COMPARISONS

I should say up front in this section that I don't believe in national stereotyping and that there is probably as much variability of board practice within any country as between different countries. However, there are cultural and legal differences between countries which do affect the way in which boards operate. Corporate history and the strength of a nation's capital markets also have an influence.

So how does the atmosphere differ?

USA

There are many things which make the way that boards operate in the USA different: the dominance of the President and Chief Executive officer role, the all-pervading influence of lawyers, the scale of ambition both personally and corporately and the culture of selling, to name just four.

In the USA the President and CEO role is effectively a combined Chairman and Chief Executive. Although there may be a chairman of the board they are very much the junior figure in terms of power and authority. It is the President who picks the Chairman, not the other way around. As one senior US headhunter once put it to me:

'No self-respecting CEO would want it any other way!'

A rules-based approach to company law has also had a big influence for good and bad, as I will describe later. When it comes to ambition there must be something in the water in the USA. The belief in what it might be possible to achieve is an endearing feature of the economy and has powered many of the world's great businesses and business leaders. Anyone who has read the biographies of the titans of the gilded age, Rockefeller, Carnegie, Ford, JP Morgan and others, knows this is not a product of the recent times but something deep in the pysche.

Perhaps the thing not much written about is what I describe as *'the culture of selling'*.

In order to explain this I need to indulge in a little political incorrectness and national stereotyping for a moment. It sometimes seems to many Europeans and Asians that Americans are genetically modified to sell. Taken positively, this is the much admired *'can do, get on with it'* attitude that has made the USA the number one economy and the superpower that it is today on so many fronts. Alternatively, it is sometimes hard for non-Americans to know where you are in the fog of bullshit. Personally I have a strong preference for *'can do'* people over *'analytical whingers'* but I have seen many occasions in the USA and outside where a team whipping itself up into a peak of *'team delusion'* could have done with a good old German or English cynic.

National traits would lead you to think that in the UK a board meeting would be a procedure-bound process and in the USA it would be a much more free-flowing 'Hi, Y'all, let's go for it' atmosphere. However, many feel that the reverse is true. Raymond Seitz, former US ambassador to the UK and an experienced board member on both sides of the Atlantic, once said:

> *'The English boards are much lighter and more fun. The US legal scene tends to sterilise a board and provides a tedious quality which it is hard to get away from.'*

*'Tom, I'd like you and your lawyer to meet my lawyer
and my lawyer's lawyer.'*

Viewing everything through the prism of potential litigation must inevitably reduce the level of risk-taking and entrepreneurial spirit for which the world admires America so much. This 'creeping legal fungus growing around a board' as Sir Christopher Hogg describes it, means that the atmosphere in the US may be much more about questioning judgements made than making them. No doubt everyone has their own favourite nutty US legal case: a popular one is the 'fast food chain sued for serving its coffee so hot you get burnt if you spill it'. My personal favourite was reported in an excellent article in the *Financial Times* entitled 'Trigger Happy Justice'. It involved a class action brought by a group of Northwest Airlines passengers for 'false imprisonment'. The basis of the claim was apparently that they were left stranded at Detroit Airport for several hours during a snow storm. Anyone seriously worried may like to feed their concern by buying a copy of *The Death of Common Sense: How the Law is Suffocating America* by Philip Howard.

Don't get too worried. I'm glad to report that there is still entertainment to be had at some US board meetings. Here are two slightly more unusual techniques for engendering a spirit of fun. The first is from the chairman of a rapidly growing technology business who:

> *"Bangs a J Arthur Rank style gong during board meetings when there is something to celebrate.'*

Amusingly his business is in mobile communications.

A slightly wackier method for which I can't imagine many takers in Europe:

> *'Before we start each meeting the President plays Aretha Franklin's 'R-E-S-P-E-C-T' on the compact disc player. Those who want to are encouraged to karaoke along.'*

Formal board meetings in the US are generally more procedural than in Europe and I can't imagine that there is too much singing or banging of gongs. Yet they do use more frequent informal and social gatherings of the board as a way of building team spirit and knowledge.

No comparison of board life involving the USA could omit the impact of the collapse of the seventh biggest US listed company Enron Inc in 2001 and the subsequent Sarbanes – Oxley act in 2002. Other celebrated governance scandals such as Worldcom and the case of domestic goddess Martha Stewart's insider dealing followed, but Enron was the key event.

The shock waves are still reverberating not just for US business or businesses outside the USA with US listings. The accounting profession has been impacted worldwide and country by country governance practices have been reviewed and amended. As one might expect, these reviews have been significant in some countries and superficial in others.

Much has been written about the collapse of Enron, which also brought its auditors Arthur Andersen down with it. Enron had become an icon of capitalist success, its sophisticated management and financial techniques much admired and its management heroes. I was lucky enough to attend a course at Harvard Business School where the Enron Chairman Ken Lay gave a very impressive speech about the company, the value it had created, the wonderful careers it had made possible and its potential. No one present would have thought that just months later his company would be one of the best known in the world for the destruction of value to customers, suppliers, shareholders, staff and pensioners and for bringing down one of the world's most admired accounting practices. Still, the lawyers got to make a lot of money again!

The political reaction to Enron was swift and strong. The US government could not allow anything so visible to undermine the moral authority of capitalism. How could it preach the benefits of *'truth, justice and the American way'* without acting? Confidence in the New York Stock Exchange and the accounting profession could not be allowed to be challenged so significantly without response. So the result was the Sarbanes–Oxley act.

Sarbanes–Oxley certainly gained the attention of all CEOs of companies with US listings. Initial reactions to use a quote of President George W Bush for a different setting (the Iraq war), were chiefly ones of *'shock and awe'*.

Maryland senator Paul Sarbanes and Ohio congressman Michael Oxley were two lawyers who were both knowledgeable and credible. They were credible to business, the Senate and Congress and neither appeared to have vested interests

So what was in their act and why the *'shock and awe'*? The Act contained a great deal of detail, as one might expect, but here are the main points in summary:

- A new 'Accounting Oversight Board' was formed under the oversight of the Securities and Exchange Commission (SEC) and accounting standards were brought under federal regulation.
- The board was given the power to enforce the professional standards designed to provide independence of firms that audit public companies.
- There were highly prescriptive new criteria for acceptable non-audit work.
- Auditors were banned from doing audits where the CEO, CFO or Chief Accounting Officer had worked for the firm of auditors within a year of the audit.

- The audit committee would now be held clearly responsible for the audit, and audit committee members were no longer allowed to collect any fees from the company other than as a board and committee member.
- The company's principal officer and financial officers are required to certify the accuracy of the financial condition of the company as presented to the SEC. The Act also mandated forfeiture of executive compensation if there is non-compliance with the Act's procedures.
- A range of additional disclosure requirements relating to off balance sheet financing, conflicts of interests and executive share ownership.
- A range of requirements in relation to stock market analysts, their independence and the disclosure of their financial interests in companies.
- The Securities and Exchange Commission (SEC) was given the power of corporate governance oversight.

One other interesting aspect of Sarbanes–Oxley was the speed with which it took effect – many of its provisions took effect immediately, the rest within 30 days. This, combined with the power and conviction of the SEC, meant that things really did change very quickly.

So how did it go down? Deciding on the appropriate response was a challenge for boards and CEOs. Any hint of challenge to the Act might be taken by the press as if you had something to hide. However, immediate acceptance made it look like the titans were either weak or didn't realise the significant increase in personal risk and cost that they were agreeing to. In the end there was a bit of behind-the-scenes lobbying and they gritted their teeth and got on with it.

What will the long-term effect be? Sarbanes–Oxley will have raised the standards of governance. It must have put some people off being outside directors and forced some high calibre managers into the arms of the willing and able private equity industry. Inevitably it will deter some companies from other countries from having US listings. And of course it has been an absolute jamboree for lawyers.

The debate stirred up by Sarbanes–Oxley also led to some challenge around the absolute power of the combined role of President and CEO and the effectiveness of many Chairmen. This, I think, will be a healthy debate long term.

France

In France the equivalent of the UK plc, the German AG or US Inc is the SA. This stands for *Société Anonyme*. Private companies are normally a Société à Responsabilité (SARL). The two main components of a French board are the PDG (*président directeur général*) and the *conseil d'administration* (the board).

A PDG is supposed to be elected by a board who have been appointed by the shareholders. In practice the PDG is king. He chooses the board and the shareholders agree. His power and authority are much wider and greater than the CEO in an equivalent UK or US business. French corporate culture remains an elitist one in which the king – sorry, PDG – and his inner circle dominate. Management styles vary but many treat their boards with complete disdain and effectively as a rubber stamp. It is a sin of course for a royal subject to put the king in a position where he has to reveal ignorance on a subject or a weakness. Loyal subjects are expected to be in position for the king's arrival, which is customarily ten to 15 minutes after the scheduled start. Their king seldom feels the need to warm up his audience with a few jokes or other pleasantries. So the start and bulk of French board meetings are serious and formal in nature.

In spite of the law requiring all companies to have a formal board and hold board meetings, many smaller and private companies, the SARLs, don't have either in practice. Because the law requires it, they tend to have board meetings which never take place. At these so-called paper meetings members of the board are just asked to vote a certain way without any previous discussion or information on the issues involved. The individual head of the company, particularly a family one, is so dominant that the function of a board has never been very important. All members of the board usually come from the same family and they are joined by the family lawyer or some other 'right hand' closely associated with the family. Communication is informal and does not usually take place in what could be considered to be a boardroom.

Le conseil d'administration for the larger businesses tends to meet less frequently than an equivalently sized UK, US or German board. Normal form is for quarterly meetings. The board must have between three and 12 members. No more than a third can be executive. PDGs have a penchant for powerful bankers on their boards. There is also a limit on the number of directorships any individual can hold. No one can sit on more than eight boards. Usually these boards are fairly passive in successful companies. Research by 3i in France showed that in smaller businesses half have less than four people on the board.

Things may be changing in the public arena in France. A series of high profile difficulties, including Vivendi, combined with institutions, politicians and journalists jumping on the worldwide corporate governance bandwagon, will undoubtedly have an impact. Combine this with the natural French love of elegance and elaboration, the domination of the state, so many proud kings and the emergence of a few queens and you can expect an interesting time ahead.

Germany

Germany has a two-tier board system. These tiers are a management board known as *der Vorstand*, which runs the company, and a supervisory board known as *der Ausfsichtsrat* in the larger businesses and the *Beirat* for smaller, private companies. Supervisory boards monitor the performance of the management board. Germany's equivalent of the managing director, president, chief executive or *président directeur général* is the *Geschäftsführer*.

There are various rules for how boards should be organised and composed depending on their position and scale. The key rules are that:

- Every AG (*Aktiengesellschaft*), ie 'share company' must have a *Vorstand*.
- A small GmbH (*Gesellschaft mit beschränkter Haftung*), ie limited liability company of less than 500 employees, may have a single-tier board with shareholder elected directors only.
- In larger AG and GmbGH seats on the *Aufsichtsrat* are shared between shareholders and employees, two-thirds for shareholders and one third for employees. These companies must have a *Vorstand*.
- Major AGs with more than 2000 employees have a similar structure to the above, but the composition of their *Aufsichtsrat* is different. Half of the directors are shareholder representatives, the others represent the employees. The chairman is always a shareholder representative.

Unlike in the UK or the USA most public companies have a dominant shareholder with a least 25 per cent of the equity. These are generally not banks as is commonly thought.

Many *Vorstände* meet once a week and sometimes for a whole day. The *Vorstand* therefore is somewhat similar to the executive committees which operate in US and English businesses. The *Aufsichstrat* tends to meet three or four times a year. These meetings tend to be highly formal affairs largely focused on compliance and legal issues with little emphasis on the strategic aspects. A cultural tendency only to speak on something if you are qualified to do so tends also to lead to statements and opinions rather than debate. The lower level of merger and acquisition activity may also reduce the need to discuss shareholder issues at the board.

The debate over whether a two-tier system is better or not hasn't really been well developed. Much of the debate has been driven by 'the grass is greener on the other side' feelings. The reality is that a dominant chairman can rule equally well under either system. Indeed if you look at the *Mittelstand,* the medium to large private German companies which are the power house of the German economy, there is no doubt that in most of them the paternalistic owner calls the shots. Moreover, a number of high-profile scandals have led to increased public questioning over whether the two-tier approach really has been as effective as it has been made out. A lack of openness combined with that natural and endearing confidence of German businessmen to have absolute faith that their way is correct has tended in the past to allow them to win discussions. It has also inhibited the self-doubting Anglo-Saxons from questioning two-tier board effectiveness.

Another feature which clearly influences the style and behaviour of German boards is that cross shareholdings between companies and between companies and banks are more common. There has therefore been a greater mutual dependency than in many other countries – a healthy state of affairs in that good relations with shareholders have been more important. Considerable help has been available when required. However, some suggest that this has inhibited change and led to a lack of clarity of purpose for many businesses. It has also meant that the bankers have been able to quietly sort difficult situations out and persuade another client to absorb a business going under before it might formally fail.

The influence of German bankers has been much written about, partly because it has been more common for the banker to sit on the board. Whilst many believe this practice is a means of bankers supplementing their income I think it has far more to do with status. A local German banker is generally more highly regarded than his English equivalent so the business is delighted to have such a prominent figure on board. The banker is equally delighted to increase his influence.

From his point of view, however, the situation has become more risky. Seeing some of your most highly regarded colleagues in the newspapers and in court over recent major collapses has clearly put personal risk on the agenda.

Other issues which will affect the way German boards are conducted in the near future are the tensions created by the need to update working practices to remain cost competitive and the obvious tensions arising from the absorption of the former East Germany. The increasing globalisation of business and the accelerating pace of merger and acquisition activity as evidenced by the watershed deals of Daimler and Chrysler merging and Deutsche Bank's difficult acquisition of Bankers Trust have had a major influence. The high profile departure of the Chairman of BMW in 1999 also added to this cultural shift and heralded an era of greater openness. For many *Mittelstand* companies there are also succession issues which, as this is often a root cause of board disharmony, should make for an interesting time ahead.

TRAINING

'Watch me doing it badly, son, and you'll learn a lot.'

This is frankly how many learn the art of the boardroom. We learn by watching and partaking with the masters and at the expense of those not so adept. We are happy to pay handsomely to invest in training for most functional and management positions. However, our willingness to invest often stops the moment people join the board. Poor differentiation between management training and director training is another frequently heard complaint. Of course the cynics believe that the majority of money spent on training is wasted and misguided.

Raymond Seitz, the former US ambassador to London, is particularly interesting to talk to on boardroom training. In making his transition from the world of government to the world of commerce and in taking up his board appointment at Lehmans he was lucky enough to have a tailored programme to ensure that not only was he well prepared for his role as a director but that he also had a good grounding in what Lehmans was all about. Lehmans organised 15 three-hour sessions on what they did and the markets in which they operate. Additional general governance and financial training was provided by Price Waterhouse.

The Institute of Directors' courses on becoming directors and the differences between being a manager and a director are generally deemed to be good value. They are also well attended by real people – an important characteristic of any useful training course.

One other aspect of training and learning naturally inhibited by the process of a board meeting is experimentation. We seem reluctant to experiment in board meetings. Having got to the board there is a natural fear of being seen to be learning or getting it wrong. The stakes are considered to be too high. This is a shame, as we might develop more as board members and as a board as a whole if we were prepared to let go and try out different approaches. Done sensibly, not only can you learn a lot by experimenting a bit, you can also have more fun and are more likely to end up more effective as a result. Just thinking about it helps enormously. Asking others how they do it is equally instructive. At 3i we have found the case study sessions for directors to be the most useful activity in this area and to be the events which have most impact, ie people develop their approach as a result.

Another easy way to develop the board is to link the review of how the board is doing with trying to give everyone on the board some educational input relating to their board role each year. One heavyweight chairman with whom I discussed this point told me that he thought this an excellent idea:

> *'But don't get too clever about it. Try and mix the basic skills such as listening with something a bit more broadening like sending your most dour FD on a one-day American-style sales skills course.'*

A ROUGH GUIDE TO HIGGS

What was 'Higgs'?

Early in 2002, in the aftermath of the Enron collapse in the USA, Marconi in the UK and other high profile corporate failures around the world, the UK Government asked Derek Higgs, a prominent city figure, to conduct a review of the role and effectiveness of non-executive directors. His report went to two cabinet ministers Patricia Hewitt (Department of Trade and Industry) and Gordon Brown (Chancellor of the Exchequer). Almost all of its recommendations were incorporated into the combined code for listed companies.

Although the review focused on larger corporate businesses, as with the earlier Hampel and Cadbury reviews, Higgs was asked to consider how any changes he recommended would impact on smaller companies.

Higgs' overall conclusion was that essentially the UK model of corporate governance was sound but there was an opportunity to improve through greater consistency of 'best practice'. He summarized what was 'best practice' in his report.

There was a very positive initial reaction on publication of the report in January 2003. Well, at least for the first few days. This, however, was then followed by a considerable and heated debate, especially over the role of the Senior Independent Director. Some of this debate was helpful and well informed and some of it was quite the opposite.

Sir Adrian Cadbury's well-accepted 'Comply or Explain' principle, which Higgs adopted, was also challenged. The principle was that there may be specific circumstances where a company can justify not complying with the code; if this is the case then the company ought to be able to clearly explain why and others can then judge whether the specific non-compliance makes sense. However, many chairmen and companies felt that the approach of the institutional shareholders, their governance officers, the voting advisory groups and the press would lead to 'Comply or breach' if they couldn't 'tick all their little boxes'. In their view the reality was that they wouldn't be given the opportunity to explain and if they didn't adhere to the combined code in its entirety they would get hassle.

Interestingly, after a period of hot debate things settled down, most of the recommendations were or are being implemented without trauma and Derek became Sir Derek.

How was the review conducted?

In a fairly straightforward and pragmatic way. In line with the Labour Government's general approach to such reviews, but unlike the preceding Cadbury, Greenbury and Hampel reviews, no formal committee was established. A small team drawn from the DTI and the Treasury was provided and Higgs could then enlist support and elicit views from a wide range of other interested parties.

His process comprised:

- Extensive research
- Formal and informal consultation
- Analysis
- Formulation of proposals
- Testing of proposals
- Presentation to Government
- Publication
- Refinement and effecting change.

The poll conducted by MORI early on in the review of 650 directors, and the census taken of UK boards, were essential building blocks in the research. The census proved especially interesting in revealing the exact demographics of UK listed company boards.

The formal consultation process elicited over two hundred formal responses. As with any consultation process, the views provided included those from the blatantly self-serving to the cunningly disguised self-serving. Happily they also included many well-balanced and helpful responses as well.

What were the main conclusions?

As has been said earlier, Higgs concluded that the basic model in the UK was sound. He found great support for the principle of the unitary board and no demand to move to a continental European style two-tier system. The same degree of consensus occurred when it came to the benefit of separating the roles of Chairman and Chief Executive.

It was no surprise that he found widespread recognition that the role of the non-executive had become more challenging and that their risks had increased ahead of their rewards. Higgs did, however, find a divergence of view on whether there was a shortage of the right people to fill these roles. Yet he did say that there may be a shortage of people willing and able to take on the role of Chairman.

He felt strongly that appointment processes could become more rigorous and transparent and that the current supply was being drawn from too narrow a pool.

Challenging the popular view that there were a large number of people holding multiple directorships, he pointed to the evidence. Only a quarter of non-executives amongst his census held more than one listed appointment.

When it came to the diversity issue he simply stated the obvious, that we have some way to go in the UK. The review by Laura Tyson from London Business School picked up this point. Yet there has been little real progress since.

On board reviews and evaluating board performance he acknowledged that this was a developing art and that there was a need to avoid a triumph of form over substance. He avoided being too prescriptive but did say that the board should state in its annual report whether such performance evaluation is taking place and how it is undertaken. So I guess we can look forward to lots of reports saying that 'The board has put in place a rigorous annual review of its performance and is supported by XX, leading firm of consultants, in the process'.

I have made reference to many of the more detailed points arising out of Higgs in the relevant places elsewhere in this book but here is a quick summary.

Higgs' recommendations

Nothing earth shattering. In summary, 'clarity'. Clarity, with respect to the role of the board and the roles of its members, clarity, with respect to appointments and processes and, finally, clarity in terms of communications between the board and shareholders.

The full review can be obtained from the DTI and the recommendations are described in considerable detail in another book by the author, *Tolley's Non-Executive Directors' Handbook.*

The main area of controversy was over the articulation of the role of the Senior Independent Director('SID') and in particular the interaction the SID would have with institutional shareholders. This and the early reporting of it got the backs of many chairmen up; who felt he was challenging their power and undermining their role, so challenged the whole thing. Further fuel was added to the fire by the suggestion that chairmen should not chair nominations committees. Once things settled down, this latter point was revised and people realised that all he was saying was that there ought to be a clearly designated senior independent director to whom institutions could go if they had a problem with the chairman.

A rough guide to the 1998 Hampel committee's report is contained in Appendix IV for reference.

What happened to his recommendations?

They were incorporated into the combined code for listed companies and to date there have been few implementation issues for companies.

During ...

'Managing the Meeting'

'The meeting will come to order.'

Responsibility for managing the process of the meeting is usually shared between the chairman and the company secretary with the latter focusing on the detailed preparations, corporate governance, compliance issues and minutes, while the chairman concentrates on the conduct of the meeting itself. My research on this subject revealed that the role of the company secretary is much underrated and there are several acting as quasi chairmen.

WHAT'S THE ROLE OF THE CHAIRMAN?

There are numerous books and papers on this subject, some of which you will find listed in the bibliography, including Sir Adrian Cadbury's excellent *Corporate Governance and Chairmanship*. I won't make any attempt to regurgitate or plagiarise them here. A few years ago I developed a menu-style appointment letter from a company to its new chairman or independent director (Appendix III). In this letter the following is proposed with regard to the role of the chairman:

- to organise the composition, business and efficiency of the board;
- to lead the board in the determination of its strategy and in the achievement of its objectives;
- to ensure the board has accurate and clear visibility of results achieved and likely future trends;
- to ensure board committees are properly established, composed and operated;
- to ensure effective relationships are maintained with all major stakeholders in the business – customers, shareholders, employees, suppliers, government, local community, industry, etc;
- to enhance the company's public standing and image overall;
- to develop a strong working relationship with the chief executive/managing director and ensure there is a clear definition and agreement of the division of responsibility.

In a private equity or venture capital context the owners would also require the chairman to:

- implement the investment and exit strategy;
- judge the executive team on their operational and financial performance;
- be responsible for management change.

SO WHAT ABOUT THE CHAIRMAN'S ROLE AT THE BOARD MEETINGS THEMSELVES?

Probably the best way to answer this question is through some observations and anecdotes on easy traps to fall into. Most of these spring out of experiences with the over-dominant. These naturally are the most memorable. However, the under-dominant or over-consensual chairman is often worse for the business.

Responsibility for the quality of the debate rests with the chairman. According to Sir Denys Henderson the chairman's role at the meeting is 'to synthesise the optimum decision from the various experts around the table'. It is not always easy for a chairman, especially one who was the builder or saviour of the business, to avoid 'being the meeting'. Despite the best of intentions it is all too easy to give out the wrong signals. The separation of Chairman's and CEO's roles is now perceived wisdom in the UK and enshrined in the combined code for listed companies. It does, however, remain a minority sport in the USA.

Sam Goldwyn's legendary quip makes the point:

> '*I want you all to tell me what you think, even if it costs you your jobs.*'

Another dramatic signal from a board that all was obviously not well between a chairman and a finance director came with the words:

> '*If I want your view, Jim, I'll ask for it.*'

Even this is better than what I heard one chairman say: 'If I want your view, I'll tell you what it is.' Generating a real debate and involving all in the discussion is quite an art.

Lord Alexander, a former barrister and therefore expert on the subject of leading witnesses, believes the best way to avoid this trap is

'Millicent, send in a fly.'

for the chairman to introduce an item briefly and with no indication of his own position. They should then set out the background, concluding with 'it seems to me this raises the following issues ...' An executive or non-executive is then chosen to present the issues more fully and lead the discussion. Only at the end of this discussion will he give his view.

Alan Greenspan at the Federal Reserve System adopts a similar approach by stating the item and asking each board member in turn to ask questions and express views. Only when everyone has had the opportunity to hear from the others are they then asked to state their position on the subject. These two are lucky not to have shrinking violets on their boards but what do you do if you have an annoyingly quiet dissenter or silent seether? How do you draw them out? I suppose you could 'just ask them what they think'. They still may be diplomatically and unhelpfully brief in response.

Highly tuned antennae and a powerful sense of intuition are handy assets for a chairman. A lovely example of this was given to me by one of the masters who wished to remain anonymous. He told me of another chairman's pivotal remark:

'I feel Martin throbbing beside me desperate to express a view.'

Once someone's discomfort with a position is picked up the wise chairman then employs additional devices to draw out the overly shy.

'Would you please elaborate on "then something bad happened"'.

Many telephone all of their board members following each board meeting to check they were comfortable with the outcomes and the discussion. Non-executive directors have to feel that this is done in a non-manipulative way. One popular variant of this approach has been described to me by one of what I call the Old Toughies as the 'behind the bike shed afterwards' approach, perhaps expressing disappointment that a board member didn't contribute at a vital moment and sending a clear signal that they will be expected to next time. Of course it can be risky to rely upon someone at a vital moment if you haven't supported them in their moment of need. Beating someone up who is already starting to introvert generally makes them retreat into their shells even further as many a bully has found out before. Really smart chairmen note the silence and have a sensible one to one later.

Another trap for those who would say 'never go in without an idea about what you want out' is either to give the impression – or worse, make it the reality – that the other participants are playing out the chairman's dream meeting. To do so is to treat them like clowns in a side show. Being a ringmaster is fun and I guess you must have a bit of that in you to want to be a chairman in the first place but if it is too orchestrated 'Why have them there?' The best example I came across of the power of a real debate came from Jon Foulds who described one of his most pleasing moments as chairman:

'Miss Howell, send in the clowns.'

'When we arrived for the meeting the night before we were all unanimous in the view not to proceed with a particular proposal. The debate at the board the following morning, however, came out a different way. Everyone was happy with the decision to proceed with the proposal. Even better, we were right to do so.'

I guess it might have been easy not to have had the discussion at the board.

For any successful team with an inspiring leader the development of an air of invincibility is an obvious danger. A team that is very well welded together might also suffer from an increasing homogeneity of thought. The feeling of being able to complete your colleagues' sentences, know exactly how they will react and so on provides some with a considerable degree of comfort. Thankfully it fills others with horror. You have to have someone who 'is prepared to water down your treacle' when things are a bit too sweet. It is always handy to have at least one person who can make things a little less cosy or perhaps even a bit uncomfortable.

Anglo-Saxon board members feel better for making a decision. There is an expectation by those putting proposals to the board that a decision will be made. Not to do so can easily be taken as a sign of weakness. In comparison, Japanese boards seem adept at delaying the decision until it is the right time to decide. Their sense of the right time is the time when the decision can be properly implemented. Allowing a decision to be made when a bit more debate or perhaps the seeking of an external view might produce a better result is an easy trap to fall into. This is not to encourage that other Anglo-Saxon trait, procrastination. A chairman's instinct and gut feel is the critical thing here. There are

Decisions, decisions

occasions where decisions are made which stack up logically, having well prepared and well argued papers to support them, but are just plain wrong. Discussions about acquisitions emphasise this point best. Sir Denys Henderson reinforced this point for me by saying:

'I've only used my chairman's casting vote twice. Both were gut-feel points against the run of the meeting and logic. In both cases I'm very glad I did.'

'I don't need this aggravation!'

'He don't need this aggravation!'

'I realise, gentlemen, that thirty million dollars is a lot of money to spend.
However, it is not real money and, of course, it's not our money either.'

That this is an American cartoon is ironic in some ways. One of the
differences between US and British boards is supposed to be the greater
emphasis in the US on shareholder issues and the greater sense, as
Norton Reamer puts it:

'... that this isn't any old company, it's theirs.'

Robert Monks, the shareholder activist who is somewhat cynical on the
subject of US board behaviour, observes that:

*'So we are agreed. Honesty is the best policy. Okay. Let's label that
Option A.'*

*'US boards talk much more about shareholder value but in practice they
aren't any better.'*

Setting the tone is a vital duty for any chairman. Alan Greenspan is
recognised as a master of this. A tone of 'serious integrity and professionalism' runs throughout his board meetings as well as his organisation. People expect an orderly consistency from the Fed. They have to
feel it's under tight control. Other organisations may want the mood to
be different but a chairman of any board has to generate an environment and atmosphere of trust as well as engender a sense of seriousness. A company's sense of integrity is easily lost by a bad example set
by the board. As a lawyer friend of mine always says:

'If in doubt fall back on the truth.'

The subject of integrity and the natural flow of dilemmas which emerges for all directors is something I've covered in another book, *Directors' Dilemmas*.

If you do have a chairman and a chief executive clarity between their respective roles is crucial. Beware of the many over-prescriptive pieces written on this subject. Gaining clarity and it working almost intuitively because of the skill sets and styles of the individuals concerned is far more important than what each person actually does. There is a body of opinion which feels that having a full-time chairman makes this potential difficulty inherently more likely to occur. Having the former chief executive as a chairman is also likely to lead to potential conflict.

'But to make a long story short ...'

Naturally a good chairman will finish on time without people feeling it's rushed or too rigid. As one football fan who also happens to be a chairman of a FTSE 100 company put it:

'A good chairman finishes on time, occasionally needing a bit of extra time to get a result in a big match. A bad one has to resort to penalty shoot-outs to get a conclusion. It's never a satisfying game for the players or the crowd if you only ever get through on penalties.'

Being a chairman is a tricky job requiring many skills. Fundamentally he or she has to command respect through former achievements. A clear mind and considerable determination will need to be matched by a keen sensitivity and openness to the ideas of others. They also need to regularly think about the process of their board and its composition. Developing the other directors is a further key responsibility. The good news is that there are many people who are first class at this and love to do it. One observation from meeting these masters in companies big and small is that they all, despite their busy schedules, have time to talk to people. When I asked how, they almost universally replied:

'Oh I'm really lucky, we have an excellent chief executive and my secretary is superb.'

WHAT ABOUT THE CHIEF EXECUTIVE OR THE MANAGING DIRECTOR?

Let's make the assumption that there is a separate and non-executive chairman of the board. There are a whole set of other issues if they aren't separate. Most people have found it very hard to make the executive chairman and chief executive combination work. Even harder, as Barclays bank found in the late nineteen nineties, to make the combination of an executive chairman, an executive deputy chairman and a chief executive work, no matter how good they may or may not be individually.

Making the clear distinction that the chairman runs the board and the chief executive or managing director runs the company is helpful. The lack of this distinction, which may exist because the chairman is weak, is often what leads to trouble. This is especially true if the chairman is weak and happy for the chief executive to run the meetings and simply feed him his lines. When the chairman is weak and unhappy for this to happen this will lead to stress for the entire board as agenda setting becomes an increasingly over-political exercise.

Before moving on we ought to address an obvious question:

'What's the difference between a chief executive and a managing director?'

I know there's been some clever stuff written about this but to an unsophisticated mind like mine it appears to be mostly semantic in nature. My own favourite definition of the distinction is: 'About fifty thousand'.

So often it really does seem to be more to do with the size of the company than the job description. Another simple distinction is that the chief executive is the executive leader of a group of companies each of which, or smaller groups of which, may have their own managing directors. In the United Kingdom the chief executive title has largely replaced the group managing director one. What remains is the variability in roles from company to company.

When I originally wrote this chapter, five FTSE 100 companies didn't have a chief executive, mostly as a result of boardroom bust-ups. The average time in their role for the top group is around four years. I wonder what you do after being chief executive of a FTSE 100?

The chief executive role has become increasingly demanding and the spotlight increasingly intense. The press have become far more interested, influential and involved in removing chief executives of high-profile companies. This means that chief executives today must pay far more attention to their relationships with non-executive than perhaps they used to. Non-executives could and have in some situations been used as the ideal conduit to a hostile press when it comes to sacking a public company chief executive. 'He no longer has the confidence of the non-executives' is becoming as popular a choice as, 'he no longer has the confidence of the institutional shareholders'.

A vicious circle can then easily develop in which the non-execs leak this to the press and then fire the chief executive because 'he no longer has the confidence of the press'. So what should the chief executive do in a board meeting given this background? Should he or she think positively and 'come to receive the endorsement and encouragement of the board and to gain useful input to their plans as well as a rigorous testing of them'? Even more so can they expect 'to be motivated by the experience'? Whatever the case they ought to feel that 'board meetings are an opportunity not a chore and that they are much, much more than an expert witness.'

Despite the appearances they may give and what they say, strong chief executives are seldom motivated by the regular show-event for the non-executives. Feeling that you made it through the meeting without much of a testing or without gaining any new input to your ideas is likely to be an unfulfilling experience. Coming away with an even-better decision or an interesting new angle and with the enthusiastic support of a bunch of tough-minded and impressive people will feel much better.

The skilful chief executive will pick up those really useful comments from the non-executives and not only incorporate them but do so enthusiastically rather than grudgingly. These are the ones that recognise that non-executives like their contributions to be recognised and acted upon just like anyone else. They avoid the trap of appearing defensive in defending a good plan. Defensiveness can easily be interpreted as an inability to listen or a reluctance to change.

How the chief executive relates to other executive board members in the meeting is another interesting topic. A chief executive who answers for the rest of his executive directors looks much weaker than the one who is very comfortable letting them join the debate without fear of loss of face. The greeting of a top chimp in a chimpanzee pack – 'Hi would you like to pick around in my hair?' – sums this up well for me. If you have decided that the purpose of your board is to get something additional from the stimulus of the debate then having others pick around the scalp of the idea might result in a better-groomed result. It also makes 'the groomers' in the pack feel closer and a lot more involved and committed to your appearance. A bunch of quiet executives throughout the meeting are as worrying as those who, leaving their strident stance at the door, have to look to the chief executive for approval to speak.

In my experience, chief executives generally have a high need for control. The time of the month when they are not in control inherently leads to tension, before, during and after the meeting. If this is combined with a chairman they fear, they are irritated by, or they simply just don't rate, then this frustration will generally find it's way into the meeting. It then becomes hard to avoid this frustration becoming destructive.

One handy tip for the chief executive who has a chairman who becomes over involved is to get the chairman busy on other things. An easy solution is to recommend them as a non-executive elsewhere. I have seen many examples of this tactic working very well for all concerned, particularly the chairman who was formerly chief executive.

It seems perfectly natural for the chairman, chief executive and company secretary to sit down together and plan how involved the chief executive should be in setting the agenda. A chairman who leaves it to the chief executive or a chief executive who isn't involved in the process is for me a clear sign that something is wrong.

The chief executive's job is the one that many people aspire to and few attain. Most chief executives I know enjoy the job and the pressure it brings and are not disappointed by it. Disappointed leaders are not leaders for long and find it hard to motivate the rest of their team.

WHAT'S THE ROLE OF THE FINANCE DIRECTOR?

Every board is fundamentally dependent upon the quality of their finance director and every board member knows how much harder the job is to do without a high quality FD. Yet how do you know you've got a good one? This is especially important to know before you join a board.

Many years ago I felt that this was an issue not being given enough prominence and so set up a series of workshops for independent directors and 3i's own investment executives. We called them *'How do you know a good FD when you see one?'* and they turned out to be very popular right across Europe. This was especially the case in countries such as Germany where historically the FD role has not had the prominence it has in the UK or the USA.

Of course, before you can determine whether you have someone who is appropriate for the role and the situation you need to be clear what the role is. So we spent some of the time establishing what the role of an FD was. There was a great deal of consistency right across Europe that the role was a combination of *'ensuring'* and *'adding value'*.

Ensuring that:

- financial controls and systems are effective;
- financial resources are appropriate to meet the company's short- and long-term needs;
- the board is made fully aware of the company's financial position and performance and has good visibility of future financial performance;
- the company has good relationships with providers of finance; and
- the financial team is appropriate and highly motivated.

Adding value by:

- being an active and contributing member of the board on issues other than finance;
- communicating well internally on financial matters so that staff had a good appreciation of the company's financial position and the impact on the company's finances of their actions;
- having a high reputation externally; and
- providing the board with insightful analysis from which to make key decisions.

What a tough job, no wonder good FDs are like gold dust.

Within the context of a board meeting the FD will frequently be the major supplier of information to the board. They are also often the major recipient of actions arising. It can sometimes therefore be hard for them to find airspace on subjects other than those relating to finance, as they will have used considerable airspace on the subject of their expertise. The best, however, overcome this and don't find it a challenge. They are also very good at both supporting the CEO and providing sufficient challenge. It is almost impossible to achieve this unless they are high calibre and high integrity.

WHAT'S THE ROLE OF THE COMPANY SECRETARY?

'As the great ones depart, and are eating their dinner
The secretary sits, getting thinner and thinner
Racking his brains as he tries to report
What he thinks that they think that they ought to have thought.'

There is much debate amongst company secretaries as to what their role is. For many, apart from the obvious formalities to attend to, 'It's what they want it to be plus the bits that the FD doesn't want to do.' Many company secretaries have greater responsibility than their title or salary indicates and have branched out into the risk management business largely through having dealt with the administration of the company's insurance policies. Some are ideally suited and well trained to deal with this new role but many sadly aren't. With regard to board meetings most of the company secretaries I spoke to suggested that their role was:

'to make the process as smooth as possible for the directors and to be their independent conscience.'

Company secretary handbooks and training materials suggest this means the following.

Before the meeting

- To notify directors of the time, date and place of the meeting.
- To prepare agenda with the chairman and then circulate it with associated papers.
- To be responsible for all the housekeeping arrangements, room bookings and preparation (including checking the clock, booking refreshments, etc).
- To advise all other relevant people (those preparing papers, information, advisers, etc).
- To organise advisers to the board. This can be particularly important especially in a flotation or bid process.
- If listed, to make appropriate Stock Exchange notifications.
- To prepare a briefing note for the chairman before each meeting, two pages in bullet point form. For formal resolutions such as share issues and so on it's normal for these to be prepared in minute form to avoid separate detailed agendas.
- On day of meeting to check again all items are covered, all papers have been made available, etc.
- To ensure any documents which might be referred to are to hand (accounts, memorandum and articles of association, etc).

During the meeting

- To be prepared to resist the temptation to speak on anything other than procedural matters. The company secretary should not be part of the discussion unless it's a procedural issue.
- To record the names of directors present at the beginning of the meeting and those that arrive or depart during.
- To check that a quorum is present and maintained, and, importantly, if one or more of the directors has an interest in an item, to check that an independent disinterested quorum is available.
- To report any apologies for absence and note them for recording in the minutes.
- During the course of the meeting, to take notes of the proceedings and of the instructions given and decisions reached. Many feel that the sense of the meeting cannot in practice be fully grasped by a person who takes shorthand notes.

- To be prepared to advise on any point of procedure. Without invitation or request to inform the chairman if any action proposed to be taken by the board is unlawful or contrary to the memorandum and articles of association or a trust deed.
- To make the precise arrangements for entry for those attendees only present for part of the meeting.
- To ensure the removal of any confidential reports or letters from the boardroom.

After the meeting

- For a listed company, to make appropriate notifications to the Stock Exchange, eg regarding dividends.
- To notify any departments or individuals of any decisions affecting them or on which they need to take action.
- To note items deferred.
- To prepare and circulate draft minutes then issue final approved minutes.

All the above sounds like a lot of hassle – why do people do it?

Some people have a natural affinity for hassle and detail and just love to organise things. They usually also have a strong belief in what they are doing and don't necessarily require the high profile and wide recognition of other board roles. Given it takes 16 exams to qualify as a company secretary in the UK these days and most qualify through part-time correspondence courses you really do have to want to do it. One company secretary told me that the job is ideal for nosey people who are good at keeping confidences. She added that the job is well worth doing for the view you get of the participants. There seems to be low mobility amongst this group and one told me that they seemed to provide another useful service – 'the continuity man and link with the past'.

It is also noticeable that whilst the proportion of women involved in most board roles is still low there is a high proportion of female company secretaries. Why is this? Of course there is ample opportunity at this point to fall into every sexist trap possible. I'll attempt to avoid this by giving you the views of some of the female company secretaries I talked to:

'Most women like to see their offspring kept out of jail.'

'Why? Because we naturally take a lot upon ourselves.'

'It is a natural role for someone with a strong maternal instinct to want to see everything in order.'

'There is a greater acceptance by middle aged men of professional women than those who rise up the ranks in a functional position.'

'A company secretary's position is an easier position to take a career break from than sales and marketing.'

THE SILENT SEETHER AND OTHER PERSONAE

The character, style and performance of any board is really established by the individuals who are on it. You may find some of the cameos below familiar. This was the part of the book most of the press picked up on when it was first published. Amusingly, I received a call from a secretary in another FTSE 100 who told me that all the board secretaries had been playing 'spot the boss'!

The silent seether

'After 34 years of marriage you thought you knew me, didn't you?
Well, welcome to the real world!'

Amongst a lot of boards you will find a silent seether. These are usually very clever, very shrewd people who sadly lack either confidence or arrogance enough to get themselves heard. Instead they sit there seething whilst others do all the talking and make the wrong decisions. Their attempts at interjecting are often too late and the momentum of the debate too great to take their view on board. Later, amongst their colleagues or at home, they vent their spleen, often threatening to resign if it happens again. Of course they never do. They just continue to sit and seethe. Until they snap.

The seether

A close relation to the silent seether, only neither as quiet or bright. Often the over-promoted insecure type they can also be known as a 'chippy' – they always seem to have a chip on their shoulder or something unnecessary to prove. A skilful chairman can use seethers to great effect. By getting them to provide an extreme version of what he wants said the chairman can get the required result with a 'That's a bit strong, Tom,' or a 'I don't feel we can go quite that far yet, Sarah.' More often than not, though, seethers just turn out to be a pain.

The key influencer

Not necessarily the chairman or managing director, perhaps a powerful family member, heir apparent, non-executive, key shareholder representative or adviser.

Mr or Mrs Wonderful

They do exist. Ideal board member material: strong views but will listen to others; questions rather than states but you know damn well where they are coming from; motivated by what is best for the board rather than their own personal position; never a slave to political correctness or to the convenient, expedient but flawed compromise; shares responsibility for a problem even when they counselled against the course of action causing all the trouble.

The quiet floater

A diplomat who never does much so has never done much wrong. A master at letting others do all the fighting and emerging the winner by making a small compromising contribution at the end, thus providing the chairman's summary and the company secretary's minute.

The dangerous ones with nothing more to offer than their silken tongues

A source of great irritation in life are those who have a wonderful capacity to sound good but aren't. Whenever they speak it sounds so convincing, so right. It's only when you stop to think, perhaps when the oozing charm has ceased and you set about trying to convert their eloquent words into action, that you realise it's complete and utter claptrap.

The really useful old hand

Always handy to have one of these sage guys around. They have seen many swings of the economic and industry cycle, survived numerous crises and had the joy of as many triumphs. They seem to possess an innate sense of when to be optimistic and encouraging and when to sound the cautionary note. Their store of general and specific industry knowledge is usually undervalued by the board. Their fierce loyalty to the inherently successful values of the business is matched by their keen sense of when it's time to change. A role for the classic coach and mentor, someone you would love to have as an uncle or aunt.

The really useless or dead hand

These sad cases have little to offer. They are usually masters from the school of decision avoidance and are fearful of anything that involves too much change or disturbance of their cosy little world. Others only tolerate them because of their shareholding or some other accident of history. They tend not to be the brightest of people and so in their desire to procrastinate they love having more explanatory information and papers to hand. Someone once said that as we get older our eccentricities become exaggerated. This lot start with a full set to begin with.

The great debater

Some people just like to talk. This group approach every issue with an open mouth and will joyfully race past the boundary of exploring the options and move out to explore the world. Board meetings tend to be much longer and as a result the other board members' attention wanes. Unfortunately this can be at precisely the wrong moment. A great appetite for the decision may then have more to do with a desire to finish the meeting than any real confidence in it.

The young pretender or heir apparent

A difficult position to get right when you are ready to assume control, it is accepted that you will be the successor but you haven't reached the formal position yet. Many an heir apparent has come to grief on the rocks of arrogance and jealousy. It is so tempting to flex your muscles and exercise that power when it isn't really yours. Others knowing it soon will be may be suitably compliant. Beware, though, because your 'Top Chimp', the person you are succeeding, may change his mind about you if you usurp his power and don't show him sufficient respect. Any heir apparent needs a mentor and a constructive critic to keep them balanced.

The pulse

This is that person who, whatever is going on, has an innate sense of what people think both inside and outside the company and how they feel. They will help the board spot the wonderfully logical decision that no one will carry out or when it is time for the mood to change. Tremendously helpful at calibrating the divisional managing director's – or baron's – presentations. Also pretty useful at dealing with the seethers.

Rosey

No matter what the issue Rosey finds a positive interpretation. Whilst they may be useful in cheering up the rest, they are typically an over-promoted super salesman unsuited to a board role.

Badvisor

This is the over-involved professional advisor who persuades the chairman that he or she should attend a board meeting as an expert on a particular issue. The board is initially delighted to have him or her come along. He or she fulfils the observer role well, contributing only on his or her area of expertise and when his or her views are sought. However, at subsequent meetings he or she becomes a complete pain.

Flushed with his or her early success, he or she starts to make uninvited contributions and talks with great force on subjects he or she knows nothing about. This person becomes known as the badvisor because of his or her capacity to cloud vision and get everyone steamed up.

All of the above explains why getting, as Lord Cuckney says, 'the right people on board' matters more than anything else. This doesn't simply mean the individuals but it also means the mix and the collective style. Get the wrong mix and watch your problems grow.

PRESENTATIONS TO THE BOARD

Presentations by non-members of the board typically fit into two categories:

'to inform, present or communicate';

or:

'to seek approval or stimulate a debate'.

You have to be clear to presenters and board members what the purpose is.

One company that is reputed to be a master of the art of making sure that presenters go away highly motivated is Mars. It seems able to do this even when those presenting get a thorough going over. Reasons given by the presenters for this are that:

'There is clear evidence that the board acts on a good proposal well presented.'

'Board members have read their papers and take you to task on all the right points. That is the most vulnerable ones or the ones you didn't even think of.'

'It scares me silly beforehand but I love it when I'm there.'

It is clear that these events fit with the rest of the Mars culture. They are therefore seen as natural and understandable. However, not every multi-national gets its logistics right, as evidenced by one horror story I was told by a company secretary of a company that claims:

'Our people are our most important asset.'

The MD of the South African subsidiary of a major UK plc was asked if he might come and give a presentation to the board. A huge effort was put into the preparation for his visit. Understandably he viewed the request as a great honour and a signal that he was destined for higher things. All his family, friends, colleagues, key customers and suppliers had been told as well. He dutifully arrived the day before the meeting to get himself settled, comfortable and further prepared. Customary practice in this company, presumably to make people feel really relaxed before they did their presentations, was to ensure all presentees were sitting outside the boardroom in an ante room at least an hour before they were due to perform. This was just in case the board arrived at the agenda item early. Our South African was due to perform at three o'clock so dutifully arrived at five minutes before two. Three o'clock passed by but at three thirty the company secretary popped out to say: 'We're terribly sorry but something's cropped up and we're a bit behind. Hang on here and I'll try to squeeze you in later.' Four, five and six o'clock came and went. At six thirty the chairman emerged and said: 'I really am most terribly sorry. We just didn't get time for you today. Something really important arose that we simply had to deal with. I hope you have a good flight back.' I wonder what impression of the board he was about to convey to his friends back home?

People understandably get very worked up about presentations to boards. For rising stars or those under threat it may be a make-or-break presentation. For external advisers, a possible opportunity to generate more from an existing client relationship or perhaps to lose it makes it a serious business.

The masters of the art were broadly unanimous on this subject and all appeared to put quite a lot of thought and effort into putting presenters at their ease. Not leaving them hanging about can be difficult if they are not invited to the whole of the meeting. One tip on avoiding this was:

'To dispense with the normal ritual of having presenters on just before or after lunch so that they can join it. Have them on first so you know they'll be presenting on time. In this way they have less time that morning to get worked up. An added benefit is that board members' attentions are usually strongest earlier in the meeting anyway.'

Another chairman always rings presenters the day before to check they are okay and that they have everything they need. He takes the opportunity to wish them well and assure them that the board is looking forward to it. He will have also given the presenter a feel for the depth of knowledge each of the independent directors has on the particular topic. A few hours after the meeting he rings the presenter to congratulate or otherwise. The same chairman is also very skilful in sheltering them a little from the more aggressive members of his board.

How well a chief executive prepares the presenter came up as an issue with most of the presenters I talked to. Other than the overconfident they all welcomed the guidance from their CEO or chairman. However, you also have to end up with something that is in the speaker's language and that they are comfortable presenting. The presenters urged 'control freak' chief executives to exercise great self-control in this area and focus on the likely discussion points arising.

DE BONO'S HATS

Sir Edward de Bono, the most celebrated and entrepreneurial of lateral thinkers, is naturally of the view that:

'Thinking is the ultimate human resource.'

However, never to be accused of being complacent, he believes that:

'most people, convinced they are competent at thinking (like humour and sex), make no efforts to improve.'

In his book Six Thinking Hats he proposed a way for any group to improve the quality of its thinking. All you need to do is to give each member of the meeting six different coloured hats. White, red, black, yellow, green and blue are the colours. Obvious isn't it?

Sir Edward recommends that you confine each stage of a discussion to thinking only from the perspective of a single colour. Each colour's perspective is as follows:

- *White.* White is neutral and objective. The white hat is concerned with objective facts and figures.
- *Red.* Red suggests anger, rage and emotions. The red hat gives the emotional view.
- *Black.* Black is gloomy and negative. The black hat covers the negative aspects – why it cannot be done.
- *Yellow.* Yellow is sunny and positive. The yellow hat is optimistic and covers hope and positive thinking.
- *Green.* Green is grass, vegetation and abundant fertile growth. The green hat indicates creativity and new ideas.
- *Blue.* Blue is cool, and it is also the colour of the sky, which is above everything else. The blue hat is concerned with control and the organisation of the thinking process, and also the use of the other hats.

The hats are supposed to allow you to think, say things you otherwise wouldn't and focus on one thing at a time. Imagine an ever-optimistic sales director doing a little black hat thinking or perhaps the gloomiest of finance directors doing a little yellow hat musing. The power is obvious and not just confined to generating a more rounded debate. Looking at things from a different perspective might actually improve the cohesiveness of the group and force the fierce defenders and promoters of their patch to be broader in their thinking.

One problem with all of this is the fact that a typical board director might feel a little silly with a bright yellow hat on. You obviously don't need to wear the hats to adopt this approach. One chairman from Scotland taken with the concept had little flags on cocktail sticks made for his board. Many of course have always tried to segment the debate at the board in a cruder 'let's look at the upside ...', 'Now what about the downside' fashion. (Those I've met who use it usually do so for the away day sessions on strategy.)

Whatever the style of your board, an experimental six-hat session would be fun and may stimulate broader debate.

SUBCOMMITTEES – THE COMMON ONES, THE RELEVANT ONES

Subcommittees of boards of larger companies enjoyed a proliferation in the 1990s. These subcommittees usually consist of three to five members of the board who meet three to four times a year normally immediately before or after a full board meeting. They can save time by being delegated the detailed discussion of technical, time-consuming, complex or less strategic but vital issues. They also allow for more considered discussion with external advisers. The balance of what is discussed at board meetings and what is delegated to these committees must be thought through carefully. Some directors see the proliferation of these committees as a potentially dangerous abdication of responsibility. Care in the drawing up of terms of reference and scope of responsibility is therefore important. As is the avoidance of stifling bureaucracy. It is all too easy to get carried away.

Many boards have established audit and remuneration committees but there are usually other ones specific to each business which can be useful. A review of the most time-consuming operational items for the board will often reveal them. For example, in 3i where our business is investing there are two subcommittees which are highly specific to our business. These are our Investment Committee and the Valuations Committee. The Investment Committee approves all investments above a certain size leaving the main board only very large investments or those which present a major policy issue to approve. A critical determinant of 3i's performance and market capitalisation is the value we ascribe to our more than three thousand investments. A special subcommittee of the board monitors both the valuation policies used and their application.

Whatever the nature of your business there are likely to be a couple of areas which can be treated in this way. Professor Jay Light from Harvard, a seasoned outside director, believes 'every board, no matter what size, should have a new products committee.' You may, if you are in oil, gas or chemicals or any other environmentally sensitive industry, need an environmental committee. In the US there has been a growing trend towards the 'strategy subcommittee of the board'.

In smaller companies with small boards and perhaps only one independent director it might seem difficult to adopt this approach. However, any smaller companies have adopted and adapted the underlying principles of delegation, specialism and planning to their own requirements and situation. An advisory board is a common technique for the smaller company to gain access to a wider pool of committed knowledge on an affordable basis. This has been especially popular in early-stage scientific businesses. Businesses making their first significant international moves may well have an international advisory board. Capturing the knowledge of people who have successfully operated in the area of interest and who are aware of the pitfalls has been the key to success for many an international foray.

Who should you pick to be on the subcommittee?

'The ones who don't volunteer.'

Clearly you must have people who ultimately do want to do it. There is value to be had by having at least one member, though, who is not an enthusiast in that area and can therefore bring some balance. For example, I think an essential member of any remuneration committee is a highly skilled communicator. Problems companies have had in this highly charged area have often not been about the levels of remuneration paid but their communication and timing.

A few remarks on the most popular subcommittees now follow.

Audit committees

The main terms of reference for an audit committee are generally to:

- review the financial statements before publication;
- consult with external and internal auditors (if there are any) regarding any matters arising in the course of the audit which should be brought to the board's attention;
- report to the board on the adequacy of internal systems and financial controls;
- report to the board on the scope of the external audit;
- recommend to the board the appointment and remuneration of the external auditors.

Another useful thing for an audit committee to do is to educate. It might be shocking to say it and no doubt many will want to lynch me for doing so, but my guess is that there is a high proportion of company directors who don't really know the basis on which their business recognises profit. A useful job for any audit committee is to make this understandable to the non-accountants amongst us. Explaining accounting policies is not easy, particularly in international businesses, but it is important. Apart from profit recognition other obvious areas for education might include stock valuation, valuation policies with regard to other assets and the level and nature of the financial risk in the business.

The management letter from the auditor always make interesting reading for a potential independent director. All too often these are confined to the finance director's file and not aired.

Understanding the real quality of the audit is much easier if you have something to compare it with. Whilst changing auditors is a hassle for a business, getting others to regularly pitch is not. Many good ideas flow from these beauty parades and if you are serious about changing, if there is good reason to, the existing auditors are more likely to provide a keener service. Internationalisation has meant that there is growing investment by a company in its auditors.

One other critical point to make in respect of audit committees is to make sure you are happy you have an effective one. Having a committee doesn't absolve you of responsibility!

Although the Higgs report stole the limelight in early 2003, another report, published on the same day and with the catchy title of 'Audit Committees: combined code guidance' was significant.

What was the Smith report all about?

Inspired by the Financial Reporting Council and led by the hugely popular and respected Sir Robert Smith, it didn't attract anything like the same debate as the Higgs review. However it was obviously less threatening to many and the attention focused on Higgs meant it received a lot less attention.

Sir Robert did an excellent job of updating best practice and the report is very clear. A very detailed analysis of it is contained in another of the author's titles *Tolley's Non-executive Directors' Handbook*. The main points the report concerned itself with were:

- constitution;
- membership;
- attendance at meetings;
- frequency of meetings;

- authority;
- responsibilities;
- reporting procedures

It was, however, disappointing to me that amongst the many skills and attributes required of chairmen and members of audit committees there was no mention of the ability to add up.

Remuneration committees

Few issues are more emotive than 'remuneration'. Potentially the most entertaining and high hassle committee to take part in on a public company board these days is the remuneration committee ('Remco'). Non-executive directors are generally keener to serve on the Remco than the audit committee because the balance of power, work and risk is more attractive.

Whether we like it or not, other people's pay is inherently fascinating to humans. Some would also say that the envy of journalists and politicians has also fuelled interest. The regular occurrence of high profile gaps between reward and performance has also ensured a regular supply of stories to feed that fascination. Journalists who cover this increasingly complex subject have become ever more sophisticated. The technical proficiency of many of them on this subject is now well ahead of the average director.

For some quoted companies the annual general meeting has become a *'remuneration issue fest'* with the preparation involved becoming enormous, much to the delight of the many remuneration consultancies and shareholder voting advisory groups now in business. There is a considerable amount of technical detail on this subject in another of the author's titles, *Tolley's Non-Executive Directors' Handbook*; however, some headline issues are covered below.

The combined code for listed companies sets out three principles on the setting and make up of directors' pay and these are:

1. Have a Remco to make recommendations to the main board on remuneration policy and to determine the remuneration of each individual director.
2. Remcos should have at least three members, all of whom should be independent non-executives.
3. The Chairman and the Chief Executive should attend the meetings by invitation only.

So if you are listed you have to have one and it is about making it as effective as possible. If you aren't, should you bother? In private equity or venture capital backed businesses the investors will normally require them. However, the constitution of decisions relating to remuneration issues is normally set out in investment agreements between management and investors. The Remco in these situations is principally concerned with benchmarking and issues relating to new joiners or exiting directors.

In owner-managed businesses there may seem little point; the owners are simply deciding whether to take their financial gain as income or capital and there is no one outside who could be disadvantaged in the process. In family businesses the same circumstances may apply but a Remco can prove to be a very helpful mechanism to satisfy non-management shareholders.

The combined code also sets out three principles for determining the remuneration of directors:

1.   Pay enough to attract relevant talent but don't overpay.
2.   Link some element of pay to corporate and individual performance.
3.   Have a formal and transparent process and don't let anyone set their own pay.

Before getting into any detail on process issues relating to remuneration a board needs to step back and have a few simple objectives. For me these are:

■   The overarching objective is to build shareholder value. Never forget that or allow anything to cloud it.
■   Remuneration policy and process should align rewards with the performance objectives of the company.

In order to achieve these objectives you will have to have schemes which attract and retain the most appropriate talent, which are market driven, are commercial and fair, comply with legal and accounting standards, avoid unnecessary complexity and finally are tax efficient for the company and the director.

A series of remuneration case studies is included in another of the author's books, *Directors' Dilemmas*. In many situations confusion arises over what is reward for a job done and what is an incentive for a job to be done. In others the confusion is around what is remuneration for a role fulfilled, and what is really a distribution to share-holders.

Terms of reference for a Remco will typically involve some or all of the following:

- Determining remuneration policy.
- Targets for performance related remuneration.
- Pension arrangements.
- Remuneration arrangements for new directors.
- Termination and compensation arrangements for departing directors.
- The individual remuneration package for each individual director.
- The preparation of the remuneration report for the annual report.
- Where remuneration consultants are used, the selection, management and remuneration of them.
- Ensuring relevant linkage with the nominations committee.

A couple of other points are worth making.

Firstly, when using remuneration consultants, never, ever choose from a choice of one; pitch it like any other supplier, manage them tightly and ensure you get a relevant firm who understands your remuneration world. The benchmarking game can easily get out of hand.

It is also important to consider the 'remuneration cycle' to ensure you have the right linkage with financial reporting. All of this takes time to plan and whoever is chairman of the remuneration committee will need to work closely with the company secretary and finance director to make this work.

The Remco chairmanship is now a serious job requiring a serious time commitment, a high degree of awareness of current best practice and a very high level of communication skills and patience. They also need, with the relevant executives, to ensure that all decisions can be communicated clearly within and outside the company, including the many lobbying and voting advisory groups which exist. Most of these bodies are highly trained, highly professional and very sensible. However, there are still many that aren't, have never been near a board-room and frankly haven't got a clue what they are doing.

A final point of commercial importance is that coming up with the right performance measures is always tricky. Worry it through, spend the time but recognise that we live in an imperfect world.

Nominations committees

The remuneration committee might be the headline grabber and membership of it may bring useful power but it is the nominations committee (Nomco) that has risen most in terms of real power over the last few years. This is largely because it was starting from almost a zero base.

If you are a listed company then the combined code says you have to have a nominations committee to lead the process for board appointments and make recommendations to the board.

In the Higgs report reference is made to the analysis and census of UK listed boards. According to this analysis almost all FTSE 100 companies in 2002 had Nomcos whereas only 30 per cent of those outside the FTSE 350 have them. He went further in his report and said that:

'Where nomination committees do exist they are the least developed of the board's committees, usually meeting irregularly and often without a clear understanding of its role in the appointment process.'

So what's the point of having one and do the big listed companies only have them because they have to?

The reality is that many listed companies do only have Nomcos because they have to. However, I believe strongly that a well-constituted and composed Nomco which has the respect of the board as a whole can add a lot of value, especially if it is advised by a high quality search firm. By high quality I don't mean that they have to be a top tier firm in the search industry. High quality in this context means highly professional, relevant and independently minded.

To have a rigorous and efficient process for picking the best people for your board that is highly defensible if challenged ought to add value. Nomcos which are a triumph of form over substance or simply rubber-stamping exercises for chairman or chief executives are a waste of effort and not worth the bother.

There has been much debate about the pros and cons of the Chairman being the Chairman of the nominations committee, and this is covered in the Rough Guide to Higgs on page 57. In my view, if the Chairman is the leader of the board team then they absolutely should chair the Nomco for everything other than the selection of their own successor. When it comes to their own successor they will obviously have significant input.

Sir Adrian Cadbury, a highly thoughtful and pragmatic man and the wise elder of corporate governance in the UK is clear what he thinks on this issue. In his excellent book *Corporate Governance and Chairmanship* he says:

> *'I believe that the Chairman of the board should wherever possible chair this committee, since it is chairmen who are responsible for the workings of their boards and who should therefore play a leading part in selecting their team.'*

The value of an effective Nomco really does come to the fore when it is dealing with the two key appointments of Chairman and Chief Executive. Most boards have a succession plan and will charge the Nomco with the responsibility of ensuring that an effective plan is in place. In order to do this they will have to have a good idea of the strengths of the existing board as well as good visibility on executives beneath the board. Today there is also the pressure from institutions, no matter how good the internal candidates are, to benchmark them against external candidates.

What about non-listed companies and smaller businesses with a small number of non-execs? In their case it is usually the major share-holder who decides, but many are now seeking external input to their decisions.

The recruitment of non-executives has become a much more devel-oped art than a decade ago. The demands of the job are much greater, as are the risks and the time commitment required to fulfil the role effectively. In public companies the nominations committee will need to plan the rotation of non-executives and in many there tends to be an appointment of a new non-executive almost every year.

In summary the role of the Nomco is changing, membership is becoming more influential but the art still has some way to go.

DEALING WITH DISHARMONY

A certain amount of creative tension and a challenging environment are healthy. Lots of companies thrive because just such an environment exists at all levels generated by the board. But sometimes there seems to be a thin line between creative tension and a right good scrap. Or worse, a whole board of silent seethers, who emerge occasionally for a sporadic outburst of violence. Why does it matter? Well, running a company looks tricky enough when the board is at the peak of its harmonious powers. Running it when it's enjoying a period of open hostility must be downright impossible. Just look at the damage to companies such as Lonrho or Cable & Wireless during their periods of painful and highly public disharmony. So it seems well worth looking at how disharmony can arise and how it might be dealt with.

Janet Morgan, a fascinating lady with extensive non-executive experience and an engagingly keen observational eye, gives a delightful talk on some aspects of board disharmony. She commences by comparing human behaviour to that of chimpanzees. After all, she says, we apparently have 98 per cent of our genes in common. Anyone who doubts this should have a look at an excellent children's book called *How to speak Chimpanzee*.

The process of a top chimp's or, sorry, chairman's succession usually provides an ideal climate for considerable disharmony to emerge. Chimps handle this in a number of different ways. An easy method avoiding any difficulty is to prepare a 'chosen one' who is demonstrably the most able of the pack and, more importantly, has their respect. In which case, apart from the tensions and sadness caused by the parting of a dearly beloved elder statesman who is wandering off to his field to die, it's reasonably harmonious.

A slightly less easy but sometimes manageable process is the warmongering 'waving of a big stick or baring of fangs' by a powerful youngster who frightens the elder in a moment of weakness. The elder quickly reaches the conclusion that it's not worth the bother fighting and quickly goes, though with not quite as much dignity as his friend who adopted the 'chosen one' strategy. Others will usually let it appear that it was the retiring chairman's idea all along. Sadly this approach may result in considerable regret a short while later. If the youngster has moved too soon or is just simply not up to the job, disharmony emerges.

Another situation arises when the elder decides to teach the young whipper-snapper a lesson on the occasion when he's cheeky enough to come along again and bare his fangs. The result this time is far more bloody. A quick resolution is all that can be hoped for but it can sometimes takes ages for a victor to emerge. When one does he and his opponent are so weakened and everybody else so fed up with the battle that the victor will only have grudging support to go with his permanent scars. It's generally not too long before someone else will take advantage of his weakened state and the inevitable mistakes made in the heat of the previous battle to effect another change.

A more abrupt but effective method chosen by aspirant successors is known as the 'coconut routine'. Here the ambitious one simply chooses his moment to lull the incumbent into a lovely and relaxing little glade.

Once he's been in there a while and the youngster has pandered to his every whim and he's become over-relaxed, the cheeky chimp suddenly leaps out from behind a tree and bonks him on the head with a coconut. A sudden and triumphant victory.

I think Janet is right that considerable disharmony arises around the time of any succession. Why? Because it's a deeply personal thing and most people who get to be on boards are almost by definition highly ambitious. This is not just about the succession of the top chimp either. The prospect of replacing any member of the team can cause similar problems. Few boards regularly do a thorough survey of top talent within and without. Understandably shareholders and others outside the business will focus their attention and thinking on the top chimp. They believe that if they get the top chimp right the rest of the pack will also be right. This is not always the case.

Another circumstance where disharmony occurs frequently is where there are joint ventures or consortium companies. These arrangements, usually born triumphantly, seldom last the course without some measure of disharmony. Neatly aligned objectives at the outset can quickly diverge. The characters thrown together are usually chosen for their technical competence or their current position, not their ability to fit with the people from the other party or parties. Hence the probability that they'll get on swimmingly in such a highly charged situation is naturally low.

Well, let's imagine you are in a tricky spot on your board, everybody seems to be fighting over the bananas and the board hasn't had the wonderful benefit of hindsight to see it coming and avoid it. Or perhaps worse, you're the one that's causing all the trouble. What can you do about it?

During a series of events on this subject I made heavy use of the advice of the Suzy Lamplugh Trust. This trust was established following the disappearance without trace of a young estate agent. Her situation touched the nation's hearts. The trust in her name was set up 'to empower all people to live safer lives'. It has done some tremendous work in raising awareness and training people to deal with the consequences of aggression. You might think this seems a bit extreme – a little bit of board disharmony is in no way comparable – but how about these little snippets taken directly from some of the Trust's excellent short guides:

- ■ 'A person on the brink of physical aggression has three possible choices: to attack, retreat or compromise [back to the chimps]. You need to guide them to the second or third.'

- 'Offer a compromise such as talking through the problem, or divert the aggression into such actions as banging the table or tearing up paper.'
- 'Try to talk things through as reasonable adults. Stay calm, speak gently, slowly and clearly.'
- 'Always respect other people's personal territory and never hide behind your authority, status or jargon.'
- 'Keep your distance and avoid looking down on your aggressor.'
- 'Avoid an aggressive stance – crossed arms, hands on hips, a wagging finger or a raised arm will challenge and confront.'
- 'Keep your eye on potential escape routes. Keep yourself between the aggressor and the door. If the threat of violence is imminent avoid potentially dangerous locations such as the tops of stairs.'
- 'Never put a hand on someone who is angry.'
- 'If you manage to calm the situation down, gradually re-establish contact. A cup of tea for each of you may cushion the aftershock.'
  And my favourite:

'Don't get in a lift with anyone who makes you feel uneasy.'

All excellent advice whenever there's any boardroom disharmony about. If this fails many of us fall back on Robert Kennedy's old adage:

'Don't get mad, get even.'

Thinking of the USA I recently found a very interesting book on a related subject. It is called *The Paranoid Corporation*. The authors William and Nurit Cohen look back at some of the highest profile major corporate crises to see what with the wonderful benefit of hindsight could have indicated that all was not well beforehand. They come from the psychologist's perspective!

They believe that problems are almost always due to two types of organisational illnesses which are easily cured once recognised:

- *psychoses:* 'illnesses in which contact with reality is lost';

- *neuroses:* 'disabling emotional disorders'.

The symptoms to look out for are some or all of the following:

- Psychoses:
  - manic behaviour;

- manic depression;
- schizophrenia;
- paranoia.

■ Neuroses:
  - neurotic behaviour;
  - depression;
  - intoxication;
  - obsessive compulsion;
  - post trauma syndrome.

I think most of us in the venture capital world would admit to not investing in someone unless at least some of the above are present!

From my own experiences manic behaviour is the one which strikes a chord in the post-disaster review. It is also often due to excessive enthusiasm following on from a string of successes. Someone, obviously a reader of the Cohens' book, once told me rather cruelly that the easiest way to spot manic behaviour is to think of a venture capitalist. The medical symptoms are:

'expansive moods, grandiosity, excessive excitement, low attention to detail and few hard plans.'

So what's the best way to deal with serious disharmony? The collective wisdom of the masters of the art on this subject seems to be:

■ At the outset observe rather than participate.
■ Find a catalyst and a galvaniser.
■ Establish what the reality of the situation is.
■ Get the participants to accept reality.
■ Gain clarity and unity of purpose.
■ Jettison those who don't share it!
■ Use strict 'rules of the game'.
■ Try a little impact therapy.
■ Recognise progress.
■ Participate like crazy!

This, I think, recognises that in a really difficult case consensus management is unlikely to work. You can't always arrange it so everyone is a winner. There are usually a significant number of losers in the process. In my experience, first-class change managers recognise this and deal with those likely to lose with considerable humanity.

Trying to act like an observer rather than as a participant is a marvellous first step. This is why people often deal with external shocks better than the slow malingering developing internal one. It is also I think a major reason why introducing someone new boosts the chances of turning a business around Someone new, no matter how rampant a doer they may be, has to look and think first before acting. It is also very difficult for most human beings to admit failure. Ditching the things they have valued or sold so highly before can be too traumatic. The emotional investment is sometimes too great. Finding and installing a galvaniser is also key. You have to have someone people will follow, particularly if it is a painful period. Those in pain and those most uncertain have to believe it will get better and that the person in charge has it under control. Many of the best galvanisers I have seen in operation also go in for what I can only describe as impact therapy.

'Catherine, have everyone stop whatever they're doing.'

If you want to make a significant change you have to get people's attention and send them very clear signals as to how serious the situation is and what new standards you want to set. In many cases this needs to be done rapidly. In such cases it is the highly visible emotive things which grab attention. These are not necessarily the most significant in cost terms but set the tone superbly.

Good examples I have heard of in severe turnarounds are:

'A new turnaround MD who ordered a car transporter for his first day and had each of the directors ceremoniously drive their new BMWs up on to it. They were replaced with much lower status cars that afternoon. In cost terms the benefit to the company was not huge. However, in the meetings later that week painful sacrifices were called for from the rest of the workforce and there was very little opposition.'

'In a company with a history of appalling cash management the new chairman demanded a fax each morning from each subsidiary managing director of their cash balance. It was easy for him to get it himself from the bank but the impact this received did focus attention on a critical feature.'

'A good way for a new CEO in a hierarchical organisation which needs a dramatic change in behaviour is to communicate directly at all levels of the organisation. Just look at what Archie Norman achieved at Asda with his "Tell Archie" campaign.'

'When I go into a company that has a history of minor improprieties which undermine the culture I fire the first person I hear of doing anything untoward. It has more impact if it is over something fairly minor. I find this quickly stops the rot.'

'Often in these situations you get a crisis of confidence. It is just as important to praise and congratulate at the same time you are beating others up. Small gestures and rewards which show your appreciation have big impact. There is nothing wrong with celebrating success even if the company overall is still in a precarious spot.'

'I get the directors to ceremoniously destroy some symbol of the past. Usually a symbol of excess. This could be anything from the fountain in the atrium to the chairman's private toilet.'

'You have to promote a junior hero as quickly as possible. Doing so emphasises that you share people's values and that there is as much opportunity as downside for people. It also helps shake up the middle rankers.'

'Get simple rules established on what it is and is not all right to spend money on. If you have made it clear and people are doing what you want, encourage them. If they are not, then fire them. The word gets around.'

'Most people grab the chequebook as soon as they get in. Of course I do that as well but it is just as important to grab the order book. No orders for anything without my say so. This also helps you to find out pretty quickly what people are committing to.'

A more in-depth treatment of conflict resolution techniques, as well as a series of case studies to practise with, is contained in *Directors' Dilemmas*, also published by Kogan Page.

After ...

'The Follow-up'

The legendary management guru Warren Bennis once said that real power was the ability to convert vision into reality. A board's real power then should be judged by its ability to convert its decisions successfully into actions. Yet when researching this book for the first time, few people talked about this aspect. The follow-up receives less attention. This chapter covers some of the issues involved.

WHAT SHOULD BE IN THE MINUTES?

Whether to record a summary of the discussion and the debate or just the decisions taken by the board seems to be a common dilemma. In the horribly litigious climate of the United States people seem to oscillate between these two positions. On the one hand the more sterile the minute the less for a lawyer to have a go at; on the other the easier a negligence suit might be. There are strongly held and differing views on both sides of the Atlantic and no clear consensus. Some adopt a traditionally neat, English, compromise and use the following style of words:

- The board took the following factors into account in reaching the decision to continue to manufacture the XYZ product following the recent leak at the ABC plant.
- The safety inspectorate confirmed the plant was made safe on DD/MM/YY. In their view the reason for the leak had been clearly identified and a number of minor procedural changes were recommended.
- A paper from the company's technical director highlighted a number of procedural enhancements which the board immediately approved.
- Workforce representatives were comfortable with the proposal to continue manufacture.
- The board also noted the positive press reporting about the company's major incident plan.
- The board wished to thank the human resources team for the way in which they provided support for the individuals injured and their families.
- The XYZ product is a long-established and significant profit earner for the group.

One of the questions I have asked chairmen and independent directors is how often they refer to previous board minutes. 'Never' was a more common response than I had envisaged. Not too surprisingly, for companies undergoing crisis 'always' was a popular response. The reasons many gave for not referring to previous minutes were twofold. Firstly their company secretary would usually circulate draft minutes for comment immediately following the board meeting. 'Immediately' typically meant within a fortnight. They would always read these and ensure that their recollection was the same as in the minutes, although the company secretaries often said:

'Few people question them and if anyone does it is always Bloggs.'

For subsequent board meetings the company secretary would normally ensure that in the preparation of papers relevant minutes from previous meetings would be noted. Most company secretaries bring relevant and recent board meetings with them to all board meetings. A number of company secretaries in larger businesses are now taking advantage of sophisticated document scanning and searching systems. For smaller companies and those less technically minded a good old fashioned indexing system seems to do the trick.

Minutes are usually written by the company secretary or in a larger business their assistant. Many now avoid shorthand for minute taking on the grounds that it encourages them to write too much. Most will circulate the minutes to all board members and those affected by a decision of the board who need to take action or be aware.

Sometimes people interpret what has been said as something quite different and the language of board minutes is an art form in itself. Here are some examples:

■ 'The board concluded that the acquisition of ABC company made an excellent strategic fit.'

or put another way:

■ *'We couldn't find any financial justification for this deal whatsoever.'*
■ 'The board had a healthy discussion over the proposed expansion of the company's plant in North Carolina.'
■ *'We had a right good punch up and no one could find North Carolina on the map.'*

- 'The board was saddened by the resignation of Mr Andrew Smith and thanked him for his service to the company through a difficult period.'
- *'Thank God he resigned before we had to fire him.'*
- 'The board approved the £100 million acquisition/buy-back of shares in the company from the market.'
- *'We've run out of ideas and leaving us with the money could be dangerous.'*
- 'After a long and far-reaching discussion to which all board members contributed it was agreed to accept the managing director's original proposal.'
- *'As the company secretary I dozed off during this debate and I knew you would do what the MD said in any event.'*
- 'Mr Zap, the marketing director, reported that the company was entering into a paradigm shift in the market-place.'
- *'There is a new product out there and we don't know what the hell is happening.'*
- 'After careful consideration the matter was deferred to the next meeting.'
- *'Too difficult to get our minds around. If we leave it for a bit it might go away.'*
- 'There was a long debate about the proposed information technology strategy. It was agreed that the auditors be asked to prepare a report verifying the proposals and commenting on the cost implications.'
- *'We couldn't understand a word of it and we'd better get someone else to give it the OK.'*
- 'The board considered the position statement from the auditors and decided that on balance taking all things into account the company met the solvency criteria.'
- *'We're hopelessly bust but we might just get saved by that big potential new order.'*
- 'Having regard to the duties imposed upon them as directors under the Companies Act and, in particular, having carefully considered the implications of the Insolvency Act, the directors unanimously agreed, in the light of the encouraging discussions held between the chairman, finance director and messrs Nat Lloyds Bank, that the company should continue to trade until such time as these discussions had inter alia been drawn to a mutually satisfactory conclusion.'
- *'The company is more or less bust and the minutes are being prepared by our lawyers in case the receivers get nasty.'*

- The chairman suggested that the board strategy away day would be more effective if held in more informal and relaxed surroundings away from the office.'
- *'Three days golf at Gleneagles – yippeeeee!'*
- 'The chairman reminded the board of the importance of receiving board papers in good time.'
- *'I don't want to see another motorcycle courier on my doorstep at 9.30 pm on a Sunday night ever again.'*
- 'In reply to the independent director's question the finance director drew attention to page 2 of the financial report and said that there had been no change from the previous occasion.'
- *'The FD wondered whether he ever read any of the board papers and indeed why he asked the same bloody stupid question every month.'*
- 'The sales director explained that the period two sales budget shortfall was due to seasonal factors.'
- *'That should hold them for a bit.'*
- 'The sales director explained that the cumulative shortfall in sales at period six masked a very encouraging picture on potential new orders for the following six months.'
- *'He's praying very hard.'*
- 'In reporting the continued budget shortfall in period nine the sales director explained that this followed the worst:

(a) Weather

(b) Market conditions

(c) Levels of consumer confidence

(d) Dumping by foreigners

(e) Strength of the currency

(f) Lack of government spending he could remember for thirty years.'

- *'Aaargh!'*
- 'The chairman welcomed the new sales director to the board and congratulated him on his proposals to totally reorganise the salesforce and distribution network.'
- *'Spotted at last.'*

HOW SHOULD THE BOARD COMMUNICATE ITS DECISIONS?

"You're fired, Donaldson!"   **"I'm sorry, I don't get your drift, sir."**

During my research it quickly became apparent that many boards were unaware of the impressions they were giving to other members of the business through the process of the board meetings. Put simply, well organised and highly effective meetings give all those who are involved in the preparation, the meeting itself or the follow-up an impression of a well organised and highly effective board. The opposite is obviously also true. A board's image is important but often only thought of in the context of its members' images.

There is no point having a board meeting which felt great, was intellectually stimulating and from which some inspired decisions emerged if you can't then put them into action because of poor communication. Sir Denys Henderson, who considers this one of the most important aspects of board meetings, uses a simple mnemonic to help him. He calls it 'The Four Cs':

Conviction: that a major course of action is right.

Commitment: from the key players in the drama is high.

Communication: about the decisions which have to be implemented.

Cooperation: from those needed to carry the decision out will be forthcoming.

Strong conviction may be displayed in all sorts of ways. The great historic leaders and business heroes have always been able to communicate a spirit of determination to achieve the desired aim no matter what the challenges or practical difficulties were at the time. This devout belief that what they are trying to achieve is 'the right thing' runs right throughout the team and is a virus which spreads like wildfire. Disbelievers tend to go quickly and quietly. Just remember the way Kennedy told the American people that they would have a man on the moon. It seems pretty clear he didn't really know whether it could be done, and there certainly wasn't unanimity over it either.

Generating and then demonstrating a sense of strong conviction from a group rather than an individual is more demanding. After all, it will often be the case that a decision to proceed with a proposal may not be unanimous whether there is a vote or not. Some chairmen will choose not to proceed if it might threaten the unity of the board. Those with strong conviction are normally very good at letting you know where they stand. They are sometimes less comfortable at letting others know where they stand.

Appropriate consultation is critical. How irritating it can be when you have had a proposal from the best performer in the business who looks to have researched it superbly before a lively and deep debate at the board approves it only to find some area of research no one thought of shows quite quickly that it's a non-flyer. There is an old chemical industry saying handy for situations when you feel things are being ill considered:

■ *'You can't build the plant and then think about the safety.'*

Consultation is important from at least two points of view. Firstly the more people you listen to who have useful knowledge on the subject the more likely you are to have covered all the angles. Secondly you are much more likely to gain the commitment and cooperation required for your chosen plan if people have been involved in helping to form it. This is perhaps why the methods used by Japanese companies to commission new plants are traditionally compared with those of Europeans. In Europe we take only two months to decide to build a new plant and then three years to build it. In Japan it takes a year to gain consensus and to reach the decision to build it, but only then a year for construction.

Commitment from the key players is much easier when there is a unity of purpose. You need to avoid the prospect of anyone leaving the board meeting and saying 'they decided'. Several chief executives I know do this by example. In a recent situation a board decided, following pressure from some of its employees, to 'get more green'. It decided to introduce several 'paper reduction strategies' immediately. This might have sounded trivial but a board is much more likely to get the commitment of others in the organisation if it too is committed to doing what matters to them.

Cooperation from your champions is achieved when they are thrilled at the prospect of carrying out the board's decision. All the other people who will get extra work or be affected need to be told in an appropriate way too. You have to get them motivated, directly or other-wise. Many boards now circulate the chief executive's report to the rest of the organisation.

A striking example of the dangers of not giving enough attention to consultation and communication with stakeholders was what happened to Shell in 2004. Failure to communicate effectively cost the chairman Sir Philip Watts his job.

BOARD REVIEW

When I wrote the first edition of this book in 1997 I wrote:

Few of us do this even though we analyse the hell out of everything else in the business in our search for higher standards and more profit. Surprising that the business process re-engineers haven't got to it yet. Or perhaps they and we think that a board meeting is such a special, mystical and inviolate thing that we shouldn't?

You get an interesting reaction when you ask people about reviewing agendas, minutes and the process of a board meeting. There's pretty well universal agreement that it's a good idea. Most people will then go on to tell you that they do it but informally and are pretty vague as to how. 'I think about it a lot on long aeroplane flights and in the bath,' one chairman told me. Another said that he wished he had the nerve 'to invite the most awkward arrogant sod in the company to review the board's process!' Amusingly when I asked him who he thought this might be he said: 'Second thoughts, not such a good idea, it's me.'

Although it would be easy to put together a Cosmopolitan magazine style 'How was it for you, dear?' questionnaire in order to get feedback, this may not be the natural medium for board members. Imagine trying to rate your partners out of ten for compatibility, the effectiveness of their boardroom foreplay, their ability to respect you in the morning or their willingness to think about safety when excited!

A more straightforward list of things to review and do might be:

■ composition of the board;
■ frequency of meetings;
■ allocation of time;
■ the boardroom;
■ what six or seven key things do we need to get right this coming year?
■ are they allowed for in the board agenda?
■ try and get to visit some other board meetings – ask them what they have on their agendas at the moment.

Pretty unsophisticated heh!

Since then the consultants have certainly moved in, much hot air has been blown on the subject, but many have recognised that there is value in conducting pragmatic reviews and the Higgs review has provided a stimulus. Overall the art of board review has moved on to a higher level and the debate has been healthy.

Two key issues for a chairman to decide when establishing a board review process are obviously what aspects will be reviewed and secondly where you want to be on what I call the 'formality spectrum'.

The way in which reviews are conducted is as important as what is being reviewed. I have seen a very wide range of approaches adopted. At the informal end of the 'formality spectrum' lies the traditional lunch with a board member where the chairman waits for the right mood and then gives a bit of feedback. If there is any negative feedback to give, it is given in coded language. At the other end of the 'formality spectrum' is a hugely bureaucratic, sterile and inefficient process involving considerable external support and cost and which somehow, despite the process, ducks the real issues.

When it comes to what to review I would tend to go back to my little triangle.

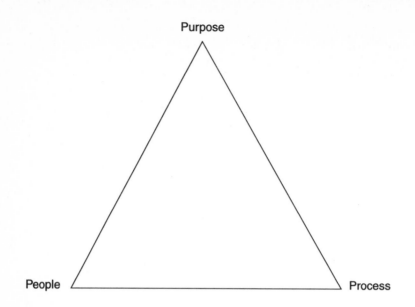

It is fairly straightforward using this to list the things you want to do under each of the headings. It should be a very quick job to review the purpose and one wouldn't expect this to change much. Most reviews will therefore tend to focus on the people and the process issues.

Many chairman have decided to take a step-by-step approach to board reviews, striking a balance between the informal and formal, and this seems to me to be the right way.

The Higgs report recommended the following with respect to board reviews:

- performance evaluation of the board, its committees and its individual directors should be undertaken at least once a year.
- the chairman should act on the results of this evaluation by recognising the strengths and weaknesses of the board and, where appropriate, appointing new board members or seeking the resignation of directors; and
- the board should state in the annual report whether such performance evaluation is taking place and how it is conducted.

In summary, 'just do it', 'act upon the result' and 'tell your shareholders how you are doing it'. No surprise then that almost 90 per cent of the 762 directors surveyed in Independent Remuneration Solutions 2005 report said that they would be conducting a review. The majority of them were on public company boards. Most of them thought that the process would take about a day for each board member time and cost more than £25,000 if they used a consultant to support the process.

As boards have experimented with different approaches a range of issues have emerged.

The quality and effectiveness of consultants in this area is highly variable. It is after all a new market and one which has attracted not just those with the requisite skills but also a bunch of people ill qualified to do the job, just looking for a fast buck. As with any consultancy supplier, the customer has to be clear what the job is, what they are prepared to pay, how they are going to manage the supplier and to conduct a proper pitch to select the right firm or individual. Many boards have used consultants simply to assist in exploring the range of approaches available, with the aim of helping them make the right selection.

For a process to be effective it must be led by the chairman, the leader of the board team. The chairman also must subject him or herself to the same depth of feedback as the rest of the team. Most turkeys don't vote for Christmas, so some chairman will inevitably feel very threatened by the idea of a board review process. The mere suggestion to some might be taken as an insult. But reviews are hard to argue against if they start in a very basic way, so in these circumstances they tend to begin with reviewing board process and duck the people issues. However, it usually doesn't take too long for the people issues to emerge. For example, common agreement that board meetings are hopelessly ineffective is giving the Chairman feedback.

On the subject of feedback I personally have a strong preference for conversation rather than questionnaire. You tend to get so much more this way. However, if the relationships aren't robust or developed, there is a place for either using a consultant to gather the feedback and play it back or for a straightforward questionnaire to be used as a first step.

There has been so much written on the art and science of 360 degree feedback processes that I won't cover it here. However, I think it is worth making the point that it is hard for someone to meet expectations if there isn't any clarity about what those expectations are. It is still the case that many non-executives don't have clear objectives. It is no surprise then that a common complaint from those departing is that '*The first time you told me what you wanted me to do was when you told me I hadn't done it*'. In my view the responsibility for establishing some good sensible objectives lies both with the chairman and the individual director.

As many listed companies are now reporting on the processes that they are using to conduct board reviews, I expect there will, like in so many other areas, be a 'norming' process that will take place over the next few years. What I hope is that board reviews will not become a chore, will not become a triumph of form over substance and will genuinely turn out to be useful things to do to add value for shareholders. Otherwise what's the point!

Conclusion

Every musician or sportsman knows that whenever they think about their technique they improve their performance. Whatever the size of your company, whether you are an experienced practitioner or aspirant, I hope that there has been something in this book that has struck a chord and provoked thought.

Appendix I:

The CHEMCO Case Study

THE SITUATION

You are the chairman of a north-west based chemicals company, CHEMCO, which has a £30 million turnover and £1.5 million profits before tax.

A regular monthly board meeting has been scheduled for 10.00 am today. Unfortunately yesterday there was an explosion at one of the company's plants. Three people were killed and a cloud of toxic gas was released causing the evacuation of local buildings within a one mile radius.

CHEMCO was established in the 1950s and has had an excellent safety record. Like many similar companies, there have been minor leakages over the years, but this is the first serious incident. There are 150 employees and the company is owned by its management (60 per cent), an institutional investor (30 per cent) and former employees (10 per cent). Of the £30 million turnover £10 million relates to a Dutch subsidiary and there is an ambitious European expansion plan.

Rather than call an emergency board meeting last night, you chose to focus on ensuring the plant was made safe, dealing with the media and personally visiting the families of those killed. You managed to speak to all the executive directors face to face and your two independent non-executive directors by telephone. The experience has been traumatic for you, your management and the employees. As yet, no obvious cause has been identified.

There are seven topics for discussion:

1. What should the agenda for this meeting be now and how long should it last?
2. What did you think of the original agenda and of the company's board calendar (see below)? What do you think an ideal board agenda should consist of?
3. Do you think the supporting information provided is adequate for this meeting? If not, what else might you reasonably require as a director of the company?
4. Describe what you think the chairman's role should be at this meeting. Who else other than the board members should attend?
5. What impression do you think the board should give to the various interest groups – employees, customers, suppliers, the media, the families involved and others?
6. Role play the meeting for 30 minutes on the attached revised agenda and then decide what you would record as minutes.
7. What subcommittees should you expect the board of a company like this to have as a matter of course and what would be their remits? Should the board establish any new subcommittees to deal with its new circumstances? If so, what and with what remits?

SUPPORTING INFORMATION

- Original agenda
- Profiles of board and key players
- MD's initial report on accident
- Sales director's report
- Technical director's report
- Board calendar
- Revised agenda (topic 6 only!)

Original agenda

AGENDA
CHEMCO Board Meeting
at 10.00 am on today's date
CHEMCO offices

1. Previous Minutes
2. Managing Director's Report
3. Finance Director's Report
4. Pricing Strategy for Next Quarter
5. Potential Acquisition for £4m of Small CHEMCO
6. Company Car Policy
7. Annual Insurance Review
8. Presentation by our Dutch MD
9. Any Other Business

12.30 pm   Lunch
               Guests: Rudi Van den Dam (Dutch MD)
               Mike Smith (Small CHEMCO MD)

Profiles of the board

Chairman	(53)	Experienced chemical manufacturing man. Early career with ICI. Joined CHEMCO ten years ago as MD when the turnover was £5 million and profits £300,000. Led a management buy-out ten years ago and became chairman. A consensus style of leader with strong communication and marketing skills.
Managing Director	(47)	Another ex-ICI man. Joined two years before the buyout as production director, became MD when the buy-out took place. A traditional, highly professional attender to detail. Very well regarded in the industry and a leading light on safety issues. Slightly autocratic and intolerant, but commands considerable respect within the business.
Finance Director	(39)	Formerly manager of the CHEMCO audit. Joined at the same time as the MD. Known within the company as Mr 'Scenario'. Always presents the options available and is a perfect judge of their outcome, but not a natural decision-taker!
Technical Director	(39)	Promoted to the board last year. Known as 'brains' throughout the company. Very bright. Has in-depth knowledge of the company's plants and processes. Less commercially adept, though wonderful with customers when explaining company's technical merits. Not generally confident when dealing with the outside world. Recently nominated as technical advisor to the Industry Safety Council.

Sales Director*	(44)	Home-grown, natural salesman. Strong on motivating the sales-force. Slightly difficult relationship with production, but wins their respect through performance rather than attitude. Particularly sensitive to the company's image and reputation.
Independent Director 1	(52)	Nominee of institutional investor. Seasoned campaigner for chemical industry who has been successful in an earlier MBO.
Independent Director 2	(54)	Previously European MD of a multinational engineering company. He is highly numerate and marketing led and is on the Board for his international management experience.

*Not on main board, but usually attends.

MD's initial report of accident

■   At approximately 10.00 am a pipe in section 16 of the main plant burst, showering a team of ten who were performing maintenance in the area with high temperature, toxic gas. Debris from this explosion also burst a nearby storage tank causing leakage of product X producing an orange, pungent cloud which, although not life threatening, caused major eye and skin irritation. The blast in section 16 could be heard throughout the plant and in our adjacent head office.

■   Buildings were evacuated (as per the regular safety training) and a bewildered and frightened staff assembled in the car park.

■   The injured were attended by first-aiders, again in accordance with procedure and training.

■   Side-effects of the leaking gas (eg severe eye and skin irritation and coughing) exaggerated the fear of a further explosion.

■   Emergency services were on the scene in minutes.

■   All mains power and services were isolated.

■   Of the ten in the area, the initial report was that the two nearest were dead, three others unconscious and the rest suffering severe shock and blast damage.

■   Gas and power officials arrived within ten minutes to assist the fire service and make safe the plant.

■   The company's lawyers provided a solicitor on site within an hour to help with employee's statements and to advise the company generally.

■   The media arrived in force with some fairly intrusive camera crews and aggressive questioning of employees: 'Whose fault is it?' 'Was this an accident waiting to happen?' etc. Distressed employees became angry at the intrusion, leading to further difficulties.

■   Two hours after the blast, the first factory inspector arrived on the scene.

Sales Director's Report

You asked me for a clear and concise assessment and some suggested actions.

- This is a major blow to our credibility because quality has been a major USP of ours and we have been able to command a high price because of our record.
- Our competitors will have a field day. We will need to cut prices to respond.
- Hopefully, the cause will be due to the maintenance contractor and we can rightly say it was their responsibility. We should change contracts immediately to reinforce this message.
- We will need the chairman to visit our top ten customers as soon as possible (ie this week) to reassure them.
- The more active PR campaign discussed at our May board meeting should be activated immediately. The best form of defence is attack.
- We must do something immediately to restore the morale of the salesforce. I suggest that the increased delegated authority proposals we discussed at the last board meeting are implemented immediately.

Technical Director's Report

- We have followed the emergency procedures to the letter and I am convinced we could not be faulted on compliance grounds.
- There must always be the possibility that the maintenance was not carried out in accordance with the procedures manual, although given the incapacity of those actually present, we just can't say at this point.
- The contractor has been used by us for the last four years. All of the contractor's staff performing maintenance yesterday were trained on this type of plant and accredited as per the contract. However, all were new to our plant. Our own trainee who was joining them as a formal part of his key programme is still in his six-month probationary period and the supervisor who was scheduled to join him was absent with flu. The stand-in supervisor decided to continue as the maintenance was classified as essential and was a routine item. I was not notified of the supervisor's absence.
- In order to help the company I feel I should resign with immediate effect and also stand down from the Industry Safety Council role. I must accept responsibility.

CHEMCO board calendar

CHEMCO Board Calendar 200*		
All meetings held in boardroom at Mills Road unless otherwise indicated.		
January 26th (Tuesday)	11.30 am	**REMUNERATION and APPOINTMENTS COMMITTEE**
	1.00 pm	**LUNCH**
	2.00 pm	**BOARD**
February 23rd (Tuesday)	1.00 pm	**LUNCH**
	2.00 pm	**BOARD** – followed by
	c. 4.30 pm	**AUDIT COMMITTEE**
March 30th (Tuesday)	11.00 am	**REMUNERATION and APPOINTMENTS COMMITTEE**
	1.00 pm	**LUNCH**
	2.00 pm	**BOARD**
April 27th (Tuesday)	1.00 pm	**LUNCH**
	2.00 pm	**BOARD** – Environmental Review
May 11th (Tuesday)	10.00 am	**ANNUAL ACCOUNTS REVIEW**
	11.00 am	**ANNUAL BONUS/PROFIT SHARE APPROVAL**
18th (Tuesday)	1.00 pm	**LUNCH**
	2.00 pm	**BOARD** – Approval of Dividend/Accounts
25th (Tuesday)		**CUSTOMER EVENT** – Paris

June
1st (Tuesday)		**AUDIT COMMITTEE**
29th (Tuesday	1.00 pm	**LUNCH**
	2.00 pm	**BOARD**

July
27th (Tuesday)		**ANNUAL GENERAL MEETING**

September
28th (Tuesday)	11.00 am	**AUDIT COMMITTEE**
	1.00 pm	**LUNCH**
	2.00 pm	**BOARD**

October
25th (evening) –		
26th (Tuesday)		**AWAY DAY CONFERENCE** Castle Howard
27th (Wednesday)	1.00 pm	**LUNCH**
	2.00 pm	**BOARD**

November
16th (Tuesday)		**ANNUAL CONFERENCE** London
30th (Tuesday)	1.00 pm	**LUNCH**
	2.00 pm	**BOARD**

December
14th (Tuesday)	1.00 pm	**LUNCH**
	2.00 pm	**BOARD**
	7.00 pm	**STAFF CHRISTMAS PARTY**

200*
Timetable of Calendar Items at Board Meetings

January   Insurance

February   Pensions

March   Environmental
                          Capital Expenditure Approvals

April   Information Systems

May   Safety
                          Balance Sheet Structure

June   Car Policy
                          Capital Expenditure Approvals

July   Marketing

August   Human Resources

September   Litigation
                          Capital Expenditure Approvals

October   Technology

November   Training

December   Capital Expenditure Approvals

Revised Agenda

**CHEMCO Board Meeting
at 10.00 am on today's date
CHEMCO offices**

■ Communications:
  - employees
  - customers
  - suppliers
  - media

■ Accident Investigations

■ Likely Financial Impact

■ Plant Re-start
  - when

■ Stock Shortages/Customer Reaction

■ Small CHEMCO Acquisition
  - press ahead or call a halt?

■ Rudi Van den Dam's Presentation

■ Any Other Business

Appendix II:

The Convo Case Study

Convo is a South Coast food manufacturing business. It was founded by its Chairman and Chief Executive, Archie Cresswell. Archie is an infectiously enthusiastic and effervescent process engineer who, over a ten year period, has grown Convo from nothing into a business with a forty million pound turnover. In the process he has been awarded a CBE and developed a profile for the business far in excess of its size. Convo has also won a Queen's Technology Award together with a string of industry prizes for innovation.

The business manufactures a mix of own label and branded products for the major UK multiple Supermarkets. It wins customers on the strength of its highly innovative way of processing, preparing and presenting its products. Three customers account for seventy per cent of sales; the balance are smaller retailers and an exciting but somewhat volatile French agent.

Archie's former employer, BigFood Co, supply most of the processing plant. They also own forty per cent of Convo through their initial support of Archie. Archie, his Finance Director, Paul Tate and the other two executive directors own fifteen per cent. Five per cent has been granted in employee shares. The remaining forty per cent is held by an institutional syndicate who invested five years ago to fund the building of a new plant. They did so in anticipation of a float three years ago.

The business has a public aura of success but the institutions are clearly becoming concerned, hence your recent appointment to the board as a non-executive director. You can understand some of their increased anxiety and have decided to jot down the following analysis:

1. The company's strategic direction is making it increasingly reliant on its few key customers. This factor also seems to be moving it closer to competing head-on with global players, such as Unilever and Nestlé.

2. Cash generative growth years fuelled by a high-margin environment are over. Surplus cash has been invested in developing new brands and building plant capacity. Recent construction of a new head office/warehouse complex has exacerbated the problem through cost overruns and disruption to deliveries. The retailers have been unsympathetic, so have the institutions with regard to deferring dividend payments. Convo is up to its overdraft limit of £8m.

3. You feel that the business has outgrown its management, which is largely inbred. Financial controls are poor, management information is over-elaborate and tends to cloud rather than highlight key issues. You are not convinced about the profitability of two of the eight key product groups. Management is demoralised by constant changes in strategic direction by the mercurial but much loved Archie.

4. The relationship with BigFood Co has become strained and less productive for Convo. Convo had to become far too involved in the detailed design of the latest machines and in fixing the considerable number of teething problems on installation. BigFood Co's new Chief Executive has allegedly been questioning the strategic sense in holding minority investments. Having said that, you are suspicious that they might be interested in acquiring control on the cheap. The Convo Board is divided into two (if not three) camps and there is much gathering of interest groups pre board meetings. BigFood Co's board representative has become evermore vocal and disparaging in his remarks.

5. This and next year will probably be loss-making given the margin squeeze from the retailers and the fact that the latest equipment is still producing at costs much higher than budgeted. There is no possibility of a claim on BigFood Co.

6. Despite all of the above, this fundamentally remains a business with enormous potential in its market and has a deeply committed and talented workforce.

Profiles of the Board members are given below. As the only independent board member, all partners (other than BigFood Co) seem to be looking to you to take the lead and catalyse the situation. You need to consider the following questions:

- What are the issues?
- How could the current situation have been avoided?
- What are the options?

Note

The articles of association for the company give BigFood Co two board votes, the institutions two board votes and management one vote. There is no casting vote for the chair. There are no compulsory purchase shareholder leaver provisions except in the termination for cause as stipulated in the service agreement of the individual director concerned. In this instance an executive shareholding may be compulsorily purchased at valuation.

Board Profiles

Archie Cresswell (45) Chairman and Chief Executive

An extreme workaholic. He loves the company – it's his baby and he knows every single employee on a first-name basis. Over the years, despite his ego, he has never paid himself adequately. Eighteen months ago the board insisted on awarding him a one hundred per cent salary increase and forced a three-year rolling contract on him. He seems a straightforward, open chap who can see that all is not well. He dominates the company, is strongly defensive of his own position and feels let down by his team. Beneath a seemingly naive and homespun exterior he can prove wonderfully adept at playing off the two shareholding factions (BigFood Co and the institutions). Domestically he is supported by a strong family who think the world of him and his achievements even though he neglects them.

Paul Tate FCA (42) Finance Director

A local man who qualified with a minor firm in the next town but got bored with auditing. Two years after qualifying he moved into broader commercial management, mostly in trading and commodity businesses. When Archie set up Convo and asked him to be Finance Director he was flattered and thrilled and considered the prospect a hugely exciting one. He did, however, have to gear up and borrow from his father-in-law to invest at the start and in subsequent rounds. A natural overcomplicator who will often miss the central point, like Archie Paul is a workaholic and is having severe problems at home. He and his wife enjoy the reflected glory of being part of the Convo success story and, despite a relatively low income, are big spenders.

Terence Foster PhD (38) Technical Director

A brilliant food technologist who pioneered the first, and still most successful, Convo product. He has always worked with Archie and has an undying loyalty to him despite growing frustration at the difficulty in finding cash to enhance the plant. Terence is financially and commercial unaware and very much the brains of the team. He hates formal presentations to investors but is always thrilled at the prospect of showing visiting buyers and the local University round the plant. He dislikes any general management activity.

Heather Brigland MBA (41) Commercial Director

Joined only two years ago from Unilever after an earlier spell at Bain and a career break. Brought in to bring more rigour to strategic thinking and planning. Sadly she has has never been able to break in to the core team of Archie, Paul and Terence and is considered and treated very much as an outsider with no influence over the board. This is a shame as intellectually she makes excellent points and if she were listened to would add a great deal. However she often tends to blow it by missing trivial practical points. She also seems to be perpetually trying to alienate Réne by scoring points.

Réne Faux (45) BigFood Co representative

Joined BigFood Co in France as a graduate the same year as Archie, although they didn't meet until they both got their first general managers jobs. Initially they got on well but once sat on the same project group and fell out violently over a redundancy programme. Réne's career faltered and he has been deeply envious of Archie's independence and very visible success. However, recently he feels he has been gaining ground and, with two highly successful acquisitions behind him, has risen to prominence within BigFood Co. He only got the board representation job at Convo when his predecessor, a former mentor of Archie's, retired. There is nothing more he would like than to put Archie in the position of having to report to him or give up his business. Archie dislikes Réne with a surprising intensity.

Angelique Beaulie (32) BigFood Co's second representative

Réne's associate. She tends to be quiet but demonstrates remarkable insight and presence when she does join in the conversation. Réne is slightly irritated by Angelique's ability to say in a few well-chosen and charming words what needs saying.

Clive Maxwell (37)

The board representative from the lead venture capital investor. Convo is his star investment and he's done much trumpeting of it inside the institution. He's becoming increasingly uncomfortable as he is out fund-raising himself and it isn't going that well. His boss has made it clear to him that if the fund-raising falls through because of problems at Convo, he won't have a job.

You – The Independent Director

A seasoned campaigner with experience of five appointments in young food companies, all of whom have experienced growing pains. You love a problem. That's handy!

Convo Subsequent challenges

Challenge one

Having stabilised the position, you decide that management has to be regrouped, and that Archie has to go. You have obtained the attached summary of his service contract. The institutions are behind you but you haven't discussed it with BigFood Co. yet.

What board process do you need to go through and what difficulties do you foresee in implementation?

Challenge two

Instead of removing Archie you decide to adopt a gradual approach and persuade Archie to bring in a new Managing Director beneath him together with a new Finance Director to replace Paul Tate. After eighteen months, Archie falls out with both of them. You remain impressed with the changes they have made.

What would you do now and what board process do you need to go through to implement your decisions?

Challenge three

The financial position deteriorates significantly and the business needs five million pounds injected. The institutional investors have been asked and they have resolved that they will only put up this money if there are management changes. BigFood Co is prepared to provide the money without changing management but insists on acquiring control at a depressed rights issue price. Archie refuses to open up the bidding to outside parties.

What would you do now?

Service Agreement

ARCHIBALD CRESSWELL (the 'Executive')
and
CONVO LTD (the 'Company')

Summary Points

Position:	Managing Director or in such other capacity as the Board of Directors of the Company ('the Board') may determine.
Period:	For three years from 31 March 200* until 31 March 200* and thereafter unless and until determined by either party giving to the other not less than twelve months prior written notice.
Remuneration:	Salary £150,000 per annum inclusive of all directors fees subject to an annual review on 31st March in each year. The Executive and his family are to be entitled to private medical insurance. In addition ten per cent of salary will be paid annually into a private pension fund. The Company will also pay for life assurance cover equal to four times salary.

Expenses:	All reasonable expenses incurred by the Executive in the discharge of his duties will be reimbursed.
Motor Car:	BMW 730i fully expensed.
Restrictions:	For so long as the Executive owns shares or is employed by the Company he will not compete with any food businesses of the Company or its subsidiaries, solicit customers or entice away employees.
	If his employment is terminated the above restrictions apply for twelve months following the date of termination.
Termination:	The Company can terminate, without notice, if guilty of material or persistent dishonesty, misconduct or serious breach of obligation, if incapacitated by illness or mental disorder or subject to bankruptcy. In such an event the Executive can make no claim for compensation.
Suspension:	If allegations arise out of serious breach of obligations, the Board can decide to suspend the Executive.
Board Appointments:	Upon termination of this agreement, the Executive resigns his directorships.

Appendix III:

The Menu Style Appointment Letter for an Independent Director

Objective: To align the expectations of the company and the independent director (ID) from the outset and set the tone of the relationship.

Method: A brief punchy letter between the company and the ID. Where the ID is a nominee there will also need to be a nomination letter from the shareholder concerned.

POINTS TO COVER

- Background to appointment
- Formality of appointment
- Basis of ID role
- If chairman, additional description of chairman's role
- How the ID will gain familiarity with the business
- Information flow
- Membership of board committees
- Meeting with auditors
- Intended term/rotation, termination process
- Time commitment

- Notification of other appointments
- Fees and how payable
- Insurance arrangements
- Independent professional advice
- Review process
- Security

BACKGROUND TO APPOINTMENT

For example: 'Following our recent MBO/MBI/raising of investment capital/acquisition of/decision to move into the German market etc the board has decided it could benefit from the appointment of an/additional independent director/chairman.'

FORMALITY OF APPOINTMENT

The board has/will approved/approve a resolution appointing you as a director; as from 1 January 200* the terms of your appointment as an independent director of this company are set out in the following paragraphs. I understand that the nominating institution has set out the terms of your nomination in a separate letter.

BASIS OF THE INDEPENDENT DIRECTOR ROLE

Independent directors have the same responsibilities to the company as any other director.

Your primary role is to:

- bring an independent and broad view to the board;
- be involved in the creation of a robust strategy;
- review and monitor the detailed plans and budgets needed to make it work.

We expect you to provide practical guidance in a wide variety of other areas including:

- being a confidential sounding board for the directors;
- enabling the board to make best use of time so that sufficient consideration is given to the development of strategy and the management structure;
- objective assessment of the company's performance and guidance on the principles of corporate legislation and compliance;
- financing;
- communication with customers, suppliers, government authorities and, most importantly, employees;
- ensuring the board has adequate systems to safeguard the interests of the company where these may conflict with the personal interests of individual directors; eg to exercise a duty to the company in such areas as board remuneration;
- ensuring that all shareholders are being provided with sufficient and timely information with which to monitor the performance of the company;
- to help ensure that the company maintains a high standard of executive leadership;
- to help ensure that the company makes and implements proper and timely plans for management successions.

CHAIRMAN'S ROLE

(ie if an independent chairman is being appointed)

- To lead the board in the determination of its strategy and in the achievement of its objectives.
- To take responsibility for organising the composition, business and efficiency of the board.
- To ensure the board has accurate and clear visibility of results achieved and likely future trends.
- To ensure board committees are established and adequately composed.
- To take responsibility for ensuring effective relationships are maintained with all major stakeholders in the business: shareholders, employees, customers, suppliers, government, industry, etc.
- To take overall responsibility for enhancing the company's public standing.
- To take responsibility for developing a strong working relationship with the chief executive/managing director and ensure there is a clear definition and agreement of the division of responsibilities.

HOW THE INDEPENDENT DIRECTOR WILL GAIN FAMILIARITY WITH THE BUSINESS

Obviously the ID will have had extensive information (written and verbal) in getting to this point so the list below is over-comprehensive.

■ We are delighted to provide you with the attached information pack containing:

    – Copies of the last five years' audited accounts, together with the management letters from our auditors

    – Management accounts for the year to date

    – A sample of our promotional literature

    – General information about the company

    – Our latest strategy (four-page business plan exec summary)

    – An organisational chart/CVs of board members

    – Our 'Who's Where' telephone guide

    – Shareholding analysis

    – Memorandum and Articles of Association

    – A summary list of our current banking covenants and the terms of investment by X

    – Papers and agenda for our last board meeting

    – List of key dates

    – Latest company newsletter.

■ During your first three months of office we would like you to visit each of our three sites and spend one day working in the business at a front-line level.

- As a first project we would like your informed views on how effective our current contract review process is.
- We would like you to take part in our Board Away Day at Noggings Hotel on 10 January 200* (papers attached).
- We would like very much, if you agree, to do a profile of you for the next edition of our newsletter. Jane Banks will be in touch to discuss this with you.

TIME COMMITMENT

Overall we anticipate two days/month after the induction phase. This will include:

- our monthly board meetings, one of which will be on the same day as the AGM. Board meetings are held at our three sites in rotation;
- our annual Board Awayday;
- half a day at our annual customer exhibition;
- the staff Christmas party!

Any time commitment above and beyond that currently envisaged will be paid for as described below.

INFORMATION FLOW

On a regular basis we would expect to provide you with:

- monthly management accounts;
- board discussion papers;
- information on any other matters material to the board.

Board agendas and related papers are sent one week in advance of each board meeting.

NOTIFICATION OF OTHER APPOINTMENTS

We will expect you to discuss potential new appointments with our chairman and keep us informed of any changes.

MEMBERSHIP OF BOARD COMMITTEES

We would very much like you to become a member of our audit/remuneration/appointments committee/s. The composition, terms of reference and recent papers of this/these committee/s are attached.

MEETINGS WITH AUDITORS

We would expect you to have an annual meeting with our auditors to discuss relevant matters. Our current audit partner is R Moxill of Grabit and Run (tel no).

INTENDED TERM/ROTATION/TERMINATION PROCESS

We are appointing you with the intention of the appointment lasting for a three-year period subject to annual review and termination by either side on a month's notice. There is to be no compensation due for loss of office.

REVIEW PROCESS

We think it would be a good idea for you and (the Chairman) to have a discussion as to how the appointment is working out after the initial three-month induction phase. Thereafter it would be good practice for us to sit down annually and discuss effectiveness. I would hope and expect in the interim if there were any matters which caused you concern about the role you would discuss them with me as soon as is appropriate for you.

FEES AND HOW PAYABLE

- The fee payable to you will be £20,000 per annum payable monthly in arrears. I understand you would like this paid to your company IND Ltd. You should submit your invoice before the 21st of each month to ensure you meet our payment run.
- Reasonable out-of-pocket expenses incurred by you in carrying out your duties will be reimbursed. To obtain payment please submit one of the attached expense claim forms.
- If you have incurred unforeseen, but agreed, extra time on our behalf over the anticipated 24 days pa, we will make an additional payment of £1000 per day.

INSURANCE OBLIGATIONS

- We expect you to make our own arrangements with regard to directors' and officers' liability insurance.
- The company purchases and maintains directors' and officers' liability insurance for all of the directors with a current indemnity limit of £10 million. Our Finance Director, John Honest, will be in touch with you to arrange details.

INDEPENDENT PROFESSIONAL ADVICE

Occasions may arise when you need to seek legal or financial advice in the furtherance of your duties. If this arises and you wish the company to pay for it you must give prior written notice to the Chairman of the subject of such advice and an estimate of the level of expenditure to be incurred.

SECURITY

Our three sites have a card security system to control entry. We would like you to have free access to the business. Could you contact our Personnel Manager, John Henry, to arrange your card?

Appendix IV:

A Rough Guide to Hampel

When was the Hampel Report?

The Hampel Committee was established through the initiative of Sir Sidney Lipworth the Chairman of the Financial Reporting council. It produced a final report in January 1998.

> *'In the wake of Greenbury's report on remuneration and at a time when the press were making serious merry over high-profile remuneration situations, the UK's Tory government was engulfed in sleaze accusations and close to breathing its last and the Labour opposition was baying for legislation.'*

What were they asked to do?

To review the findings of the Cadbury committee on Corporate Governance and the Greenbury committee on Remuneration. Then to concentrate on how these findings might be implemented. Their work was aimed at publicly listed companies.

> *'Pull all the previous stuff together, recommend a code of conduct and save the government legislating.'*

Who was on the committee?

The sponsors were the London Stock Exchange, The Confederation of British Industry, The Institute of Directors, The Consultative Committee of Accountancy bodies, The National Association of Pension Funds and the Association of British Insurers. Sir Ronald Hampel, the Chairman of ICI, a FTSE 100 business that although strategically challenged was known for doing things properly, led the committee. Sir Ronnie was widely considered to be a sensible man, balanced politically, effective behind the bike sheds and a good chairman. He was joined by: Sir Nigel Mobbs and Sir Clive Thomson to give the views of big business; Michael Coppel, Chairman of a small plc, to act as the voice of smaller businesses; Giles Henderson, Senior Partner of leading city law firm Slaughter and May, and Peter Smith, Chairman of accountants Coopers and Lybrand, Tony Richards from Henderson Crossthwaite and David Thomas from Equitable Life to give the shareholders perspective; and Tom Ross from Aon to provide expert remuneration input.

'That should keep everybody happy.'

What did the final report say?

In summary nothing much new and certainly nothing controversial. It simply pulled it all together quite nicely. Correctly it started by reminding us that, 'the primary purpose of business is to create wealth', a point which was in danger of being lost as the corporate governance bandwagon rolled on. Another excellent point, which did get a little lost, was that there was strong support for the unitary board in preference to a two-tier system. The report raised the shareholder responsibility issue that the institutions should stop whingeing and start acting by voting.

It reinforced the view that disclosure was more powerful than legislation and that principles were more important than guidelines. I suppose one way of expressing this is to say that what boards did was more important than what they said they did. As the report only costs £10 (see bibliography) I will only comment on the principles here.

So what were these Principles of good corporate governance?

These related to Directors, Directors' remuneration, Shareholders and Accountability and Audit.

Directors

The board. Every listed company should be headed by an effective board which should lead and control the company.

> *'Better start with a safe statement of the bleeding obvious.'*

Chairman and chief executive. There are two key tasks at the top of every public company – the running of the board and the executive responsibility for running the company's business. A decision to combine these roles in one individual should be publicly explained.

> *'We don't think it's a good idea to have a combined Chairman and Chief Executive but we've got a few mates or clients who seem to do it rather well.'*

As less and less PLC's combine the role this is dying as an issue in the UK.

Board balance. The board should include a balance of executive directors and non-executive directors (including independent non-executives) so that no individual or small group of individuals can dominate the board's decision taking.

> *'We found this one tricky. We're not sure whether the non-execs should be in the majority so we copped out. Wonder what the definition of dominate is?'*

Supply of information. The board should be supplied in a timely fashion with information in a form and of a quality appropriate to enable it to discharge its duties.

> *'Wow!'*

Appointments to the board. There should be a formal and transparent procedure for the appointment of new directors to the board.

> *'The Chairman or Chief Executive decide between themselves. There should be a proper selection process. We all know that whatever formal process is put in place, a Chairman who wants his mates appointed will get them through it, thus ending up with a board that will continue to let him do what he likes.'*

Re-election. All directors should be required to submit themselves for re-election regularly and at least every three years.

'We all know that if you want to get rid of someone the re-election process isn't the way.'

Directors' Remuneration

The level and make-up of remuneration. Levels of remuneration should be sufficient to attract and retain the directors needed to run the company successfully. The component parts of remuneration should be structured so as to link rewards to corporate and individual performance.

'Look, we know most reward schemes reward strong performances in good businesses if they join and cash in at the right times in the cycles of their industries and economies. We also know that the lucky weak guys get rewarded for being there at the right time as well. It isn't so bad either for the unlucky weak guys who get found out. They command a premium to go. We really wish it wasn't like this but we can't come up with anything better.'

I write the above as the Chief Executive of a well-known group in the UK is reportedly being paid almost £1.5m as a pay-off. The value of his group is the same as when he joined over five years ago.

Disclosure. The company's annual report should contain a statement of remuneration policy and details of the remuneration of each director.

'Wish we were remuneration consultants or printers.'

Shareholders

Shareholder voting. Institutional shareholders have a responsibility to make considered use of their votes.

'Stop whingeing and start voting but don't give the gun to the trigger-happy people who don't have the competence.'

This is an area where surprising progress has been made, most notably in the celebrated case of Lucas Varity. Here was a case where a company's dominant Chief Executive was soundly beaten in his objective to move the domicile of the business from the UK to the USA, the cynic would say to be closer to his main house.

The dilemma was that his record was strong but what he wanted to do looked wrong. Large- and small-shareholders, who I'm sure a few years earlier wouldn't have bothered, rejected the proposal. Don't feel for the guy too much though, the outcome was that the company was put into play, an auction proceeded and he made a small fortune from his options.

Dialogue between companies and investors. Companies and institutional shareholders should each be ready, where practicable, to enter into a dialogue based on the mutual understanding of objectives.

> *'An index investor is an index investor. A FTSE 100 company is a FTSE 100 company.'*

Evaluation of governance disclosures. When evaluating companies' governance arrangements, particularly those relating to board structure and composition, institutional investors and their advisers should give due weight to all relevant factors drawn to their attention.

> *'Committee-speak worthy of an EEC communiqué.'*

The AGM. Companies should use the AGM to communicate with private investors and encourage their participation.

> *'We know the institutions find analyst meetings more helpful. Yet the rigour of having to prepare for the eclectic and often spot-on questions the private shareholders ask is, we believe, worth hanging on to. This is despite the fact that for some companies the cost of mounting the AGM is greater than the combined value of the shares of those attending.'*

Accountability and Audit

Financial reporting. The board should present a balanced and understandable assessment of the company's position and prospects.

> *'We haven't anything new to say to this.'*

Internal control. The board should maintain a sound system of internal control to safeguard shareholders' investment and the company's assets.

> *'Or this.'*

Relationship with auditors. The board should establish formal and transparent arrangements for maintaining an appropriate relationship with the company's auditors.

'We're nearly finished now.'

External auditors. The external auditors should independently report to the shareholders in accordance with statutory and professional requirements and independently assure the board on the discharge of its responsibilities under financial reporting and internal control above in accordance with professional guidance.

'Hooray we've done it.'

What was the reaction?

Big business: *'Sounds sensible. We won't be hampered by Hampel.'*

Politicians: *'Boring issue now we've got more interesting things to think about.'*

Press: *'Not a lot to have fun with.'*

Smaller businesses: *'Not much in here for us, this is for the big boys.'*

Advisors: *'Yippeeee, more fees for helping people to read it and to show that they are complying.'*

A Rough Guide to Greenbury

The main thrust of the Greenbury report in 1995 was concerned with disclosure and accountability. Emphasising fairness and balance is inherently difficult in these documents. They did, however, state:

> 'UK companies mostly deal with directors' remuneration in a sensible and responsible way.'

> *'Keep this in perspective – most of us are good guys.'*

Another quote from the Introduction:

> 'The detailed provisions have been prepared with large companies mainly in mind, but the principles apply equally to smaller companies.'

> *'Our brief is to look at the big boys. We don't know too much about the little guys anyway. However, most of what we've come up with seems like common sense to us so it probably applies. In private companies the executive directors are probably the shareholders as well, so if the shareholders are being ripped off they are ripping off themselves.'*

The code itself contains nine key points on the remuneration committee:

1. To avoid potential conflicts of interest, boards of directors should set up RCs of non-executive directors to determine on their behalf, and on behalf of the shareholders, within agreed terms of reference, the company's policy on executive remuneration and specific remuneration packages for each of the executive directors, including pension rights and any compensation payments.

    'Self-regulation by executive directors on pay doesn't look to have worked so let's leave it to the non-executives. All right, the executives have traditionally picked the non-executives and there are many cross-directorships. We are, however, placing the responsibility and the spotlight on the non-execs who have more to lose than to gain by getting it wrong. We've also spotted that selective disclosure has hidden the level of true benefits.'

2. RC chairmen should account directly to the shareholders through the means specified in this code for the decisions their committees reach.

    'If there is the possibility that they may have to stand up at the AGM and defend their decisions they'll take it seriously. All right, we know that only a small proportion of shareholders turn up at AGMs. However, institutional shareholders are becoming sporadically more interested and active on these issues with varying degrees of ability and common sense.'

3. Where necessary companies' articles of association should be amended to enable RCs to discharge these functions on behalf of the board.

    'Better make sure they've really got the legal power to act.'

4. RCs should consist exclusively of non-execs with no personal financial interest other than as shareholders in the matters to be decided, no potential conflicts of interest arising from cross-directorships and no day-to-day involvement in running the business.

    'Just to make it clear, we mean the real non-execs.'

5. The members of the RC should be listed each year in the committee's report to the shareholders. When they stand for re-election the proxy cards should indicate their membership of the committee.

'Don't try shooting them quietly or sticking poodles up.'

6. The board itself should determine the remuneration of the non-executive directors including members of the RC within the limits set out in the articles of association.

'This should avoid the executives getting their own back.'

7. RCs should consult the company chairman and/or CEO about their proposals and have access to professional advice inside and outside the company.

'This is not just emotive, it's technical and tricky and you do need some calibration with what everyone else is doing etc. You don't want to dream it up in a short meeting half an hour before a full board meeting begins.'

8. The RC chairman should attend the company's annual general meeting to answer shareholders' questions about directors' remuneration and should ensure that the company maintains contact as required with its principal shareholders about remuneration in the same way as for other matters.

'We'd better repeat point 2 just to make it clear!'

9. The committee's annual report to shareholders should not be a standard item of agenda for AGMs. But the committee should consider each year whether the circumstances are such that the AGM should be invited to approve the policy set out in their report and should minute their conclusions.

'Some of us wanted to go even further.'

The proposed terms of reference of a remuneration committee in the Greenbury report are fairly broad and therefore easily adapted to any size if it is appropriate to have a remuneration committee in the first place. They are:

■ To determine on behalf of the board and the shareholders the company's broad policy for executive remuneration and the entire individual remuneration packages for each of the executive directors and, as appropriate, other senior executives.
■ In doing so, to give the executive directors every encouragement to

enhance the company's performance and to ensure that they are fairly but responsibly rewarded for their individual contributions.

- To comply with our code of best practice!
- To report and account directly to the shareholders, on the board's behalf, for their decisions.

Bibliography

Brassey, Richard (1995) *How to Speak Chimpanzee*, Orion Publishing Group Ltd, London

Cadbury, Sir Adrian (1990) *The Company Chairman*, Director Books, Fitzwilliam Publishing, Cambridge

Cadbury, Sir Adrian (1992) *Report of the Committee on the Financial Aspects of Corporate Governance*, Gee Publishing Ltd, London

Cadbury, Sir Adrian (2002) *Corporate Governance and Chairmanship*, Oxford University Press Ltd, Oxford

Charkham, John (1994) *Keeping Good Company*, Oxford University Press Ltd, Oxford

Cohen, William and Cohen, Nurit (1993) *The Paranoid Corporation*, Amacom, New York

De Bono, Sir Edward (1990) *Six Thinking Hats*, Penguin Books Ltd, London

De Vries, Manfred Kets (1995) *Life and Death in the Executive Fast Lane*, Jossey-Bass Publishers, San Francisco

Dunne, Patrick (1992) *Increasing Calls on Independent Directors: A 3i Analysis*, 3i plc, London

Dunne, Patrick (1994) *Angel Investors: A 3i Analysis*, 3 plc, London

Dunne, Patrick (1995) *Running Board Meetings: A 3i Analysis*, 3i plc, London

Greenbury, Sir Richard (Chairman) (1995) *Directors' Remuneration: A Report of a Study Group* (The Greenbury Report), Gee Publishing Ltd, London

Hampel, Sir Ronald (Chairman) (1998) Committee on Corporate Governance, Final Report

Higgs, Sir Derek (2002) review of the role and effectiveness of non-executive directors

Hodgson, Phil and Hodgson, Jane (1992) *Effective Meetings*, Century Business Publishing, London

Howard, Philip (1996) *The Death of Common Sense: How the Law Is Suffocating America*, Warner Books

Independent Remunerations Solutions (2005) *The Independent Chairman and Non-Executive Director Survey.* Independent Remuneration Solutions, 9 Savoy Street, London WC2R 0BA. Tel: 020 7836 5831

Jack, Andrew (1993) *Audit Committees: A Guide for Non-Executive Directors*, Accountancy Books in association with The Board for Chartered Accountants in Business

Lorsch, Professor Jay (1989) *Pawns or Potentates?*, Harvard Business School Press, Boston

Semler, Ricardo (1993) *Maverick*, Century Publishing, London

Stuart, Spencer (1995) *Board Trends and Practices at Major American Corporations*, 277 Park Avenue, New York NY 10172

Suzy Lamplugh Trust (1995), *Personal Safety at Work for You*, The Suzy Lamplugh Trust, London

Top Pay Research Group (3i Independent Directors Programme) (1999) *The Independent Chairman and Non-Executive Survey*

Index